APPLETON-CENTURY PHILOSOPHY SOURCE-BOOKS

Sterling P. Lamprecht, *Editor*

WRITINGS ON POLITICAL PHILOSOPHY

BY

BENEDICT DE SPINOZA

WRITINGS ON POLITICAL PHILOSOPHY

BY

BENEDICT DE SPINOZA

Edited by
A. G. A. BALZ
University of Virginia

D. APPLETON-CENTURY COMPANY
INCORPORATED
New York   London

NOTE

THE translation of the *Tractatus Politicus* and of the selections from the *Tractatus Theologico-Politicus* employed in this volume is that of R. H. M. Elwes, Bohn's Philosophical Library, Chief Works of Benedict de Spinoza, London, 1883. The courtesy of George Bell and Sons of London in permitting the use of this translation is gratefully acknowledged. Unless otherwise indicated, quotations from the other writings of Spinoza are drawn from the Elwes translation.

A few changes have been made in the translation of Elwes. Here and there a word or phrase has been altered, and on occasion the Latin has been inserted in parentheses in the text, or has been given in foot-notes. With respect to Elwes's foot-notes, some have been omitted, some retained without change or extended, and others replaced. Spinoza's own notes (in the *Tractatus Theologico-Politicus*) are indicated by giving his name in parentheses at the end of each. The Latin insertions have been drawn from the Gebhardt edition of the *Opera*.

The purpose of this volume is to provide under one cover the body of Spinoza's writings on political philosophy. It appeared impracticable to include the whole of the *Tractatus Theologico-Politicus*. Portions of this work, however, are indispensable to the story of Spinoza's political thought, and selections from this tractate are therefore included. The tractate serves a two-fold purpose: in certain chapters and portions of chapters, Spinoza deals with matters of genuine political import; in the remainder of the work, he is concerned primarily with a literary criticism of Scripture, with the interpretation

v

of Hebrew history and the religious content of Scripture. This criticism of Scripture and these interpretations may be regarded as consequences, applications, and illustrations of Spinoza's political thought—of his metaphysical, ethical, and political philosophical ideas. Only those portions of the *Tractatus Theologico-Politicus* in which Spinoza is dealing with political theory have been selected for inclusion in this volume. In view of the importance of Spinoza's notion of faith, of the distinction between faith and philosophical thought, and of the proper content of the universal religion, the preface has been reprinted and extended by a note containing lengthy citations from Chapter XIV. These selections from the *Tractatus Theologico-Politicus,* added to the *Tractatus Politicus,* thus provide virtually everything written by Spinoza on political theory.

The editor desires to express his obligation to Dr. W. S. A. Pott, President of Elmira College, for a number of helpful suggestions. To my colleagues Mr. L. M. Hammond and Mr. W. S. Weedon I am indebted on this as on so many other occasions. To Mr. Iredell Jenkins, duPont Research Fellow in Philosophy in the University of Virginia, I owe thanks for relieving me of the burden of proof-reading.

A. G. A. B.

CONTENTS

vii

CHAPTER X. OF ARISTOCRACY (*conclusion*)

CHAPTER XI. OF DEMOCRACY

I

THE *Tractatus Theologico-Politicus* is justly regarded as a document of the first importance in the establishment of the Higher Criticism. The larger portion of the work is indeed a document of this character. But Spinoza's attempt to study Scripture as literature is really incidental to his main purpose, as its sub-title indicates. Here is a fact of the utmost significance. The problem of political philosophy, so Spinoza evidently thinks, cannot receive an unambiguous treatment until the nature and function of religious belief shall have been determined. And this, in turn, depends upon an estimate of the real purport of Holy Writ. Accuracy of estimate can be attained only when the scriptural documents themselves are studied in their own terms, independently of the fund of tradition springing from this religious literature. The teaching of the documents themselves, as distinguished from the dogmatic and theological structures anchored upon them, must be discerned. The sacred writings must be viewed apart from institutional interests and the accretions of history. In the *T.T.-P.* the Jewish-Christian "revelation" is studied. It is obvious, however, that Spinoza's point of view and purpose would apply in principle equally to all religions and their sacred lore.

The basic problem of political philosophy is that of Authority or Sovereignty. The medieval age bequeathed to modernity precisely this problem of authority—in the field of science and philosophical speculation, in religion and theology, and in political theory. The vast attempt at synthesis associated with the name of St. Thomas Aquinas—despite its continued influence within the modern intellectual tradition—was not accepted as a definitive solution. The political and religious turmoil of the Age of the Reformation, together with the revival of Platonism and the intensification of the scientific movement, inevitably centered Spinoza's attention upon the problem. To distinguish religious belief from dogma, positive or sacred theology from rational theology, the individual as possessed of religious convictions from religious institutions and organizations, the content of a universal religion from the content of the various historical religions, the attitudes and activities dictated by religious belief in its purity from the consequences of scientific and theological speculation—all of these, in Spinoza's view, must precede a direct treatment of the political problem. Only by accomplishing this preparatory work, given the total conditions of the age, could Spinoza attain his purpose of setting forth "That freedom of thought and speech not only may, without prejudice to piety and the public peace, be granted; but also may not, without danger to piety and the public peace, be withheld." By this procedure alone, Spinoza believed, could he approach the problem of Authority and construct a rational politics.

The State represents a principle of authority. For Spinoza, a dual sovereignty of Church and State would be an impossible conception. The separation of Church and State is for him an unintelligible phrase. In so far as by "Church" is intended something institutional, some form of human organization with its governing rules and authoritative governing body, there can be no Church at all save as an incidental component of the totality of social organization. The State, however, is in

some sense coterminous with social organization. In whatever
sense a "Church" may legitimately exist, it lies under the
authority of the State. There is, accordingly, no legitimate
problem of determining the respective places of Church and
State. Rather, for Spinoza, this pseudo-problem is resolved into
a real problem, that is to say, the task of distinguishing religion as such from its associated elements and then of determining its true function both in relation to and in separation
from the State. For Spinoza, then, a distinction must be drawn
between religion in its genuine essence, on the one hand, and
everything that may be comprised within the field of organized
action and observance, on the other. Religious faith must be
defined in such a way as to prevent its confusion with the
many elements with which it has been historically associated.
It must not be confused with the various historical expressions
of religious insight, with their accompanying and merely historical details. It must be kept apart from dogmatic formulation, from ecclesiastical organization. It must be distinguished
from its various historical institutional embodiments. Finally,
religious faith must be recognized as something wholly dis-
tinguishable in principle from scientific and theological speculation. In a word, faith must be separated from religious
institution, and religious belief from organized action. It is evidently Spinoza's conviction that faith itself is essentially a
matter of ethical illumination. It is, moreover, his conviction
that there is a single universal faith variously expressed in every
historical religion. This faith can be, so to speak, disentangled
from what are really merely associated elements. Faith, in this
sense, would define the content of a universal religion. Indeed,
it should be possible to express such a content in a few words
of universal acceptability. All that lies beyond this is subject-
matter for scientific and philosophical speculation. It is therefore wholly unnecessary for a State to place its power in sup-

port of one effort of speculative theology, just as it is wholly improper for the State to support one scientific hypothesis as against another. In so far as this universal faith can be defined, and in so far as this faith is expressed in action, there can be no conflict between religion and the State. The activities demanded by the universal religion must inevitably be acceptable to the State, and indeed cannot fail to be in essential harmony with the ideal functions of the State. There is, then, no place for a Church as a Power or Authority within the State, or coördinate with the State. There can be no dominion within or alongside of the dominion of the State. In the end, if Spinoza's thought be pushed to its ultimate conclusions, his political doctrine must become a Rational Theocracy.

The aim of religious faith is obedience, Spinoza reiterates. This means the realization in action of a few fundamental ethical principles. Beyond this, the State can have no interest whatever in the details of individual religious belief, as it can have no interest in the details of theological or scientific speculation. It is to be noted that Spinoza's doctrine would not so much exclude as reduce to mere practical devices the details of religious institutional organization, the historical content of religions, and dogma. These details must be regarded in a wholly pragmatic way. Spinoza, one infers, might well recognize that the less enlightened would need the support of formula and institution. So long as such supports are taken to have a merely practical value, they may well be tolerated by the State. Ideally, universal religion, together with science and rational theology, would render unnecessary the precipitates of emotion and imagination in dogma and creed, in institution and dogmatic theology. Given the limitations of humanity, however, dogma and creed and institution may be needed, just as perceptive and perceptual imagination, rather than the intellect, are indispensable for the many.

We must not conclude that Spinoza recognizes no limits to the authority of the State. On the contrary, he perceives that there are limitations springing from two sources. One set is defined by the structure of human nature and of nature as a whole. The other limits have an ideal source. The activities of men, since they occur within space and time, and are movements of matter, are subject to control by the exercise of superior force. In metaphysical terms, a thing's being is its power. In a world of things, each thing asserts its being subject to the being of other things equally assertive of their existence. Human beings are just so many things. Human action, therefore, is controllable directly by the exertion of superior force. It can be checked or deflected precisely as the movement of a stream of water can be checked or deflected. All that is needed is the employment of appropriate measures. Granted this, however, there is a portion of human activity that escapes direct control. Inner states or psychological conditions—passion, intellectual processes, mental attitudes, convictions—are not controllable in specifically determinate ways by external agencies. It is sensible to forbid by law this or that act expressive of the hate of one man for another. Given the efficient exercise of force, it is possible to prevent such acts, or at least to inflict punishment if they occur. It is possible by public action to reward and to encourage by reward the performance of defined activities. The motivation of these activities is not, however, directly governable. It is foolish to declare by law that men should love one another; to forbid envy, hate, and greed; or to demand by law that a man should be convinced of this philosophical position, of that religion, or of one rather than another scientific generalization. Thus nature and human nature—in a word, Nature—sets limits to the reasonable exercise of authority.

Such statements, it must be acknowledged, require serious

qualification. Within limits not easily determinable, passion, attitude, thought process, and conviction are controllable. In so far as environment is a factor in the organization of the inner life, in so far as physiological and similar factors are determinable of mental process, in that measure an oblique control is feasible. The exercise of authority may govern the press, the educational means and agencies, and an enormous variety of conditions that contribute towards the upbuilding of the self. Propaganda, in an extended and complete sense of the term, is far-ranging in its influences. The limits of control, of effective and definitely guided control, by such means must remain uncertain. The most thorough and dictatorial supervision of environment must reckon with the incalculable resources of human nature, with its spontaneities and unpredictable reactions. In any case such control is not merely indirect but external. In the end its effectiveness is negative rather than positive. The governors of a State, for example, may eradicate all of those influences that would make the citizenry specifically Christian rather than Mohammedan, or specifically Mohammedan rather than Christian. It may well be doubted, however, whether the control of mind by governmental authority can ever be more than uncertain and haphazard.

However this may be, the natural limitations upon the governance of mind are reinforced, in an insuperable degree, by ideal demands. It may be urged that, for Spinoza, the complete governance of individual minds by the State is an impossible task. This is true, not for reasons of ignorance, physical limitations, or lack of power, but for reasons of principle. If the governors of the State fail to recognize the prerogatives of reason in the individual, the State is destroyed. To invade mind with alien power, to deny the integrity of the rational self, to withhold freedom of thought and speech,—this would be a denial of the life of reason itself, and the destruction of the State. The State and the Citizen are conjoint expressions of the Life of Reason. Propaganda, in the vicious and extended sense of the term, is a denial of reason in the Citizen, and in consequence it contradicts the very idea of the State. Where there are no Citizens, there cannot be a State. In so far as the governors of the State violate the prerogatives of reason, in that degree the Citizen loses citizenship. At the limit, the Citizen disappears and there remains a herd of bipeds, definable as human only in a biological sense. At the limit, Society vanishes, and the State is non-existent. It is for this reason that Spinoza gives to the final chapter of the *T.T.-P.* this title: "That in a free state, every man may think what he likes and say what he thinks." The adjective "free" is indeed redundant.

II

Spinoza's political terminology—to-day more frequently ridiculed than understood—is characteristic of his age. Beneath his usages, however, lies a metaphysics extraordinarily compact in expression and illimitable in vision. It may be contended that Spinoza's metaphysics was designed to support his ethical doctrine. It is equally sound to contend that Spinoza's political philosophy, even though his terminology is shared by others, is a structure of ideas consistent with his metaphysics. Many typical statements on the political theme, however, may astonish and mislead the reader who is unacquainted with the metaphysics. His terminology, taken unguardedly, seems to express a morally ruthless and offensive attitude. The unwary reader feels a marked contrast between the aspirations voiced in the first paragraphs of the *Emendation of the Intellect,* the lofty heights of the *Ethics,* and the doctrine of right and power in the political contexts. The difficulties in understanding Spinoza's political doctrines cannot be easily dissipated, and certainly not within the limits of an introductory note. These difficulties, however, may be alleviated if their sources are recognized.

The similarities between the political philosophies of Spinoza and of Hobbes are well known. In the final analysis, these similarities may well mask ultimate divergencies reflecting metaphysical differences. However this may be, Spinoza and Hobbes share a common fund of terminology. Natural Right and Civil Right, the State of Nature and the State, the Compact or Contract with which the State comes into being— these and related expressions suggest a similarity of approach to the political problem. But these terms are ambiguous; to the later reader they may obscure rather than illuminate the general mode of analysis pursued by Hobbes and Spinoza. Two reasons for this may be assigned. The first reason may be described as the reader's failure to recognize the presence of two contexts or levels of discourse. By the contrast and interplay of these two contexts the terminology receives intricate definition. Unless these contexts are explicitly defined, the characteristic terms of Spinoza's doctrine are systematically equivocal. The second source of misunderstanding may be described as the apparent historical connotation of the terminology.

The language of Hobbes and Spinoza (and of Rousseau, for that matter) suggests an historical approach to the study of Society and the State. The doctrine of the formation of the State by compact suggests a series of historical tableaux. Men first live in the State of Nature. The State of Nature is a condition of war, the *bellum omnium contra omnes* in Hobbes' picturesque phrasing. Then, after sufficient experience of this war, with an accumulation of wisdom born of perpetual conflict, the State is formed. Individual men, coming together, enter into a mutual contract. They surrender their Natural

Rights, transfer their Natural Right to the Sovereign, and so the State with Civil Right and Sovereignty comes into being. Now it may well be doubted whether a Spinoza or a Hobbes was concerned with the history of humanity. Historical tableaux, at best, could scarcely do more than serve an incidental purpose in an essentially analytic procedure. Perhaps Spinoza and Hobbes deliberately adopted quasi-historical language as a literary device. The student of Locke discerns a similar question with respect to the 'origin' of knowledge. If the reader of Spinoza and Hobbes be unwilling to concede that the historicity of terms was for them merely a device, no harm is done if the historical suggestions be neglected. The essential procedure and thought of Hobbes, for example, is certainly more accurately grasped when the tableaux are laid aside. The State of Nature, for example, is not the concept of a biological condition or stage in human evolution. To ask whether men ever lived in a state of war of each against every other is really an irrelevant question. The concept expressed in the phrase "the State of Nature" is functionally of extreme importance. The expression is intended to convey a concept defining the limits of analysis. The State of Nature may be taken to mean the condition of social disorganization. In so far as society is disorganized, in that measure men live in the State of Nature. Since society is nowhere perfectly organized, every so-called historical State—Athens or Rome, the Egypt of the Pharaohs, indeed, all of the 'States' that have existed or now exist—are really hybrids. Within them men have lived or now live simultaneously in the State of Nature and in the Civil State. This suggests that the preceding definition of the State of Nature is inadequate. As defined by the essential doctrine of Spinoza and of Hobbes, 'social dis-organization' is a contradiction in terms. Society is organization: where, then, there is disorganization, there and in that measure society does not exist, there and in that measure the State cannot be discerned. The meaning of such statements cannot be wholly intelligible until the distinction of contexts to which reference was made above shall have been accomplished. For the moment it must be urged that Society and the State, for Hobbes and Spinoza, mean organization—organization in a certain sense and at a certain level—or they mean nothing at all. Granted this, it is clear that the State of Nature functions primarily in a negative sense. It defines, by negation and abstraction, the meaning of Society, of life when veritably human. Beginning with Society and the State, the State of Nature brings analysis to an end. The war of each against all makes manifest the significance of political and ethical obligation. As analysis discloses what constitutes Society and the State, so analysis simultaneously discloses what does *not* constitute these—and this is the State of Nature.

The imaginative content ascribed to the State of Nature is of relatively little importance. Whether it be portrayed as war or peace, as the uncontrolled expression of a ruthless selfishness or as a golden age of innocence expressing a human nature uncontaminated by civilization, depends upon the view that may be taken regarding the psychological constitution of man. Given Hobbes's convictions concerning the motivation of human behavior, the *bellum omnium contra omnes* is a singularly appropriate metaphor. Given another view, it might well be utterly inappropriate. In the language of Spinoza, the State of Nature corresponds to Human Bondage in the *Ethics,* the bondage that obtains when Reason is an instrument of passion and subserves the interests that are animal. How men may pass from war to peace, from hate to love, from bondage to freedom —here Hobbes and Spinoza may differ. But that men are men only in so far as this transition is accomplished—here there is a fundamental agreement.

With this, however, we are directed towards the other sources of misunderstanding. This was described as a failure to discern two contexts or levels of discourse. The treatment of political problems is marked by a continual shifting from one to the other context. It is noteworthy that Spinoza himself has suggested the two universes of discourse within which his thought moves. In the fifth chapter of the *Tractatus Politicus* he writes: "When, then, we call that dominion best, where men pass their lives in unity, I understand a human life, defined not by mere circulation of the blood, and other qualities common to all animals, but above all by reason, the true excellence and life of the mind." "Reason," following the phraseology of the paragraph, denotes one of the two contexts. Life defined by qualities common to all animals suggests the other. The term "nature" more than any other conveys the systematic ambiguity generated by a movement from one context to the other.

In the language of the *Ethics,* the contexts might well be designated as Bondage and Freedom. For the reader unacquainted with Spinozistic metaphysics, it may be simpler to describe the one context as scientific, the other as supra-scientific. More specifically, the former might be called the universe of discourse pertaining to biological science, provided we give to biology an extended meaning. If this be accepted, the contrasted context might well be described as supra-biological. There is a difficulty, perhaps even a begging of the question, in using such designations. The terms, it must be acknowledged, suggest a consistent systematic structure that science in general and biology in particular may not possess. The science that we call 'modern'—or sometimes, with eulogistic intent, merely 'science'—continually breeds reactions against its own dominant tendency. This science has been characterized, in the main, by a tendency to eschew teleological explanation.

Final causes, purpose, are denied a functional rôle in the inventory and organization of the subject-matter. Perhaps it is true that this denial has been more consistently proclaimed than observed. Under various guises—within the distinction between structure and function, for example—teleological explanation, one suspects, has been surreptitiously employed. The perennial conflict between the mechanist and the vitalist in biology suggests that neither the subject-matter nor the conceptual structure of biology has been definitely determined. Moreover, this conflict within biology is but a part of a more general struggle. Descartes, who wished to define the basis and principles of an all-comprehensive science of nature, provided an organized statement of the characteristic drive of modern science. But the Cartesian complement to—or rather, the basis of—a universal mechanistic science was a rational theology. In the development of modern science, the Cartesian and Spinozistic bases were forgotten. In consequence, the term 'natural science' suggests a consistency scarcely justified by its procedure and the formulation of its issues. From these considerations, it is obvious that the phrase 'the context of natural science' is not without its own ambiguity. In the light of the Cartesian-Spinozistic ideal, however, the ambiguity is removed. The rejection of teleology within the domain of a universal science of nature, on the part of Descartes and Spinoza, is comprehensible only within their metaphysical views. After all, Spinoza's acrid critique of final causes is a critique not of teleology as such but of an inadequate teleology springing from a confused metaphysics. With these precautionary statements, however, we may be content with the position that Spinoza envisages a non-teleological science. Following the Cartesian view, for Spinoza biology is but a chapter in the vast book of a universal physics. Within this physics final causes are function-less. The subject-matter of this science is indeed precisely that which can be described as the State of Nature.

To conceive of man in the State of Nature is then to place him within this ordered scientific context. It is to be noted that man, not a part of man, must be comprised within this network of ideas. In the useful terminology of Aristotle, man possesses a vegetative, an animal, and a rational soul. Man is a rational animal, but not a reason. Man is not a rational soul but an animal that characteristically and distinctively includes this soul. This point has importance. Man is not an animal to which something beyond is added; it is, on the contrary, man-as-possessing-the-rational-soul that is an animal. Accordingly, man with all three of his 'souls' falls within the scope of a complete biological science. The powers that we call 'intellectual,' the faculty described as 'intelligence,' are within the biological context just so many functions. It may or may not be the case that the man-animal possesses such powers while other animals do not. This must be determined in just the way in which biology must determine whether all animals have the capacity for flight. From the biological standpoint, to assert that man possesses intelligence is in principle as simple a statement as this, that fish have the power of swimming. Just as 'by nature' man is said to have the power of locomotion or of digestion or of respiration, so in an identical sense he has 'by nature' whatever powers may be signified by intelligence.

Within the biological scheme are included, we may assume, the effects of the environment upon the living thing and the effects of the living thing upon the environment. The subject-matter of that chapter in biology which concerns man is therefore, in some sense, coterminous with all of human life. Because some animals have the power to burrow in the earth, for that reason the consequences of this power are discoverable in field and wood. Indeed, within the context we seek to describe, the animal burrow and the human habitation are much the same thing. As with the power of burrowing, so with the powers of intelligence: the traces of the latter may be found wherever the human animal has sojourned. Spinoza, like Aristotle, does not mean that man is an animal having a supra-animal function of intelligence. Rather he means that man, being the animal that he is, is an intelligent animal. It may well be the case, as we shall see, that because man is an intelligent animal he must be studied within an additional context of ideas. The completed biological science of man, if achieved, would be just as complete as the completed biological science of other living things. Yet this science, when completed, would not be the whole study of man.

In the State of Nature, then, and in the framework of natural science as conceived by Spinoza, all of man and all of the consequences of his powers are comprehended. But if this be true of the individual animal, it is equally true of the facts and consequences that accrue from the association of these individuals. The career of the man-animal, biologically surveyed, presents an intricate system of interactions between individuals. Other man-animals condition the activities of a given man-animal, or of a group of man-animals, just as directly as inanimate objects condition these activities. Living things are certainly masses of matter in motion, whatever else they may be. The collision of a man and an inanimate object and the collision of a man with a man are quite similar phenomena. Man is a herding animal. The life of the kind is congregate— a characteristic shared by some other kinds. Society and the State are indeed concepts lying outside the biological context. Their meanings are irrelevant to the conceptual scheme of an extended biological science. The irrelevance, however, is of context, not of factual material. This, indeed, is precisely the reason why the 'State' and the 'State of Nature' are opponent ideas. In the biological context, we must conclude, it is as natural for men to live in groups of varying complexity, to have an ordered congregate mode of existence, as it is natural for bees and ants to exist in communities. Biological concepts, as a Descartes or a Spinoza would have defined them, do not disclose Society and the State, but they do disclose that the unity of the herd pertains to the human kind.

Within the context so indicated, descriptive differences are discernible, but not a hierarchy of worths. The biologist, if he be faithful to this context, cannot ask whether one form of congregate life is better than another. One kind of ant may exhibit one form of congregate life, another kind a different form. Since both occur, they are equally natural. The entomologist may indeed inquire as to whether the one form is 'higher' or 'lower' in something called an evolutionary scale, whether one is more or less successful than the other. But such phrases, if we do not surreptitiously pass out of our context, have no normative meaning. If the biologist think in terms of adjustment to the environment and the survival of the fit, he will discover no occasion for esthetic appraisal or ethical evaluation: at least no Cartesian-Spinozistic biologist would feel the need. Spinoza, in a famous passage, declares that he will consider human actions and appetites just as if he were considering lines, planes, or bodies. Within the State of Nature there is nothing to deplore and nothing to cause rejoicing.

This detached neutrality of biology, it must be noted, applies equally to the manifestations of intelligence within the herd life. Doubtless the herd life of animals possessing intelligence differs from the herd life of animals not owning this capacity. We must not surreptitiously import a new order of meanings into what must be regarded as a merely descriptive difference, for if we do we shall have deserted the State of Nature. The herd life of man may not be explicable save by reference to powers of intelligence; in a similar way, the group life of ants may not be explicable save by reference to some power, a peculiar power of sense, let us say, found in ants but not in man. There is in this nothing to evoke astonishment. We expect fish and fowls to live in different ways because fish and fowls are unlike in this or that respect. The exercise of intelligence by the individual may have 'survival value.' Such exercise may have survival value for the continuity of the herd in time. So, for that matter, thickness of hide or furry covering may increase the chances of survival. The herd that by concerted action tramples to death the predatory animal may have a better chance for continued existence in time than the herd that disperses. In an identical and equally neutral sense the human herd by concerted action may preserve its existence. Within the context of the State of Nature, however, if we be consistent, adaptation and survival, the serviceability of intelligence, are merely descriptive phrases pointing to causal components. The wages of sin may be death. This may have a salutary meaning for a biologist, for even biologists fall within a context other than the State of Nature. For biological science, however, the proposition merely suggests the complexity of causation within its province. A biologist may regret the extinction of the dinosaurs. But this regret is a subjective sentiment pertaining to the man and not to the scientist. Living exemplars of the extinct kind might facilitate inquiry, if the scientist wished to study this fragment of his subject-matter. In a quite similar sense, he might regret the passing of the human race, if perchance he preferred to study man rather than beetles.

This context, so defined, supplies one set of meanings for the terminology employed in Spinoza's political theory. Spinoza asserts that the bigger fish eats the smaller fish by supreme natural right. In a like manner, the stronger man—stronger by virtue of muscle or cunning—has natural right to whatever his strength may enable him to secure. Right and power—in a more usual formulation, right and might—are identical. Within the State of Nature, within the scientific context, Right is either irrelevant or it is equivalent to power. Natural right *is* power, and nothing more, whatever in the human kind are the sources of power. If human life be construed in the State of Nature—within the competence of biology—nothing as such has priority over anything else. Whatever happens, by virtue of the fact that it does happen, is right and natural in this sense of the term. Crimes that within a different context may be described as 'unnatural' are in this sense wholly natural. Nature comprises everything that in point of fact does occur or can occur. If the larger fish eat the smaller by supreme natural right, then by parity of reasoning it follows that the stronger human herd may conquer and subject the smaller herd by supreme natural right. Within the context of nature so defined, natural right, natural obligation, and natural necessity are identical terms. Everything that exists, because it exists, strives to remain in existence. Right, obligation, necessity can mean nothing more than this. In a world comprising, amid its innumerable things, such things as human animals and herds; in a world comprising things animate and inanimate in prodigious abundance; in this world the collisions that arise from the innumerable claims to existence are all equally within nature. This is the State of Nature. With reference to the human animal, the State of Nature is the life of man as an incident within the total stream of events.

It was suggested that a biologist might regret the extinction of the human race, but only for reasons of sentiment or subjective desire. The extinction of this form of life, like the passing of the dodo, would indeed mean the loss of a portion of biology's living subject-matter. Moreover, and incidentally,

there would then be no biologists to investigate any part of
biology's subject-matter. In one sense this is a trifling fact. In
another sense, however, it is symptomatically important. It suggests that within some other context man and biologists and
biological science must be integrated. It indicates that animals
possessing intelligence are one thing, but animals possessing
biological science are another. It was not for lack of reasons
that medievalists, picturing the scale of beings, placed men
(including the biologists) between the animals and the angels.

It is obvious that Spinoza's terminology, when obtaining its
meaning from the preceding universe of discourse, is free of
evaluative meanings. The equivalence of natural right and
power is not an ethical but a pre-ethical statement. In the State
of Nature, the bigger fish that eats the smaller, the stronger
man that destroys the weaker, equally escape praise and blame.
They neither are what they should not be nor are what they
should be—they merely are. The fish and the man act from
the necessities of their natures within the necessities of an all-
comprising nature. In the State of Nature, right and wrong in
the ethical sense, truth and falsity in the intellectual sense, are
meaningless. Indeed, the State of Nature is what it is precisely
because these distinctions are irrelevant.

It is to be noted that human intelligence itself defines the
State of Nature. The human intellect, in other words, views
the whole of nature and so must view itself as a part of nature.
Mind, organizing the system of ideas that for Spinoza describes
the State of Nature, recognizes that mind itself must fall
within this context. But the mind, in recognizing this consequence, while including itself within the subject-matter of a
complete biological science, achieves something not unlike a
miracle. It detaches itself from nature—from the State of
Nature—in order that it may survey a defined subject-matter.
But with this accomplishment, the mind perceives the necessity

for another context for discourse. With this transformation
scene from fairyland the intellectual powers of man take on a
new significance. Hitherto we have used the term 'intelligence'; but now Spinoza's own term, Reason, becomes more
appropriate. Man, by virtue of his rational powers, discovers
himself to be rational. The intellect with which man is endowed is no longer *my* or *our* reason—it is Reason. Within
the State of Nature—for the Spinozistic biologist—the powers
of intelligence are in subservience to the biological process. But
when Reason defines the State of Nature, it discloses another
life of man, the Life of Reason. Reason, even when taking
account of intelligence as a biological function, must reckon
with itself. Reason discovers that it is evaluative. It distin-
guishes the true from the false. It establishes canons of correct
thinking. It defines a life for man in accord with Reason and
subject to the imperatives of Reason. For Aristotle the rational
soul is the distinctive attribute of man. The life of man must
remain animal, for it cannot be other than the life of the man-
animal. It can be distinctive, however, only when it exploits its
distinctive power. This is possible only if Reason assays its own
nature, and discloses to itself and so to man that which Reason
is. In the measure in which this is achieved, in that degree the
life of man is transformed into the Life of Reason.

Here, then, emerges a second context of discourse. It was
suggested above that it might be described as supra-scientific.
In a sense, indeed, it might be described as supra-natural, in
that it is above and nevertheless comprehends the State of
Nature. The State follows upon the State of Nature, Civil
Right supplants Natural Right, Obligation supervenes upon
Necessity. This is the transition from one context to the other.
With the transition, the term 'nature' takes on new meanings.
It is not Spinoza's intent to deny that Society, the State, Civil
Right are natural. They are indeed supra-natural in the sense

in which the term is definable in the first context. But if it be true that man by nature possesses a rational soul; if it be true that Reason itself has a 'nature' (for it is what it is); if it be true that man, becoming cognizant of Reason, must acknowledge its authority, then Society, the State, Civil Right, and Moral Obligation are natural. They are natural for they are indeed nothing more than aspects of the Life of Reason. Within the State of Nature it is impossible to discern these things, just as within it we cannot discern freedom but perceive human bondage alone. To pass from this to another context is to pass to the Life of Reason because of Reason's demand that life be in accord with Reason. Spinoza—and Hobbes for that matter—really mean that the State implies the organization of human affairs in terms of a rational principle or idea. The sovereignty of the State is the sovereignty of the principle. As the individual must pass from herd-membership —that is, from the State of Nature—to the Life of Reason, so the herd life must pass from the State of Nature to the State that is governed by Reason.

This so-called passing, of the individual and of the herd, from the State of Nature to the State of Reason is not an alteration of 'facts.' It can scarcely be regarded as an addition to the sum of facts concerning human life. The transition is a movement to a new point of view. The data of the State of Nature are to be reexamined. The State of Reason designates the system of concepts upon which the reëxamination is based. Within this new context of thought there is no escape from principles of valuation. Civil right, sovereignty, justice and injustice, law, social order, the social and the anti-social—these and similar terms imply tests or standards of estimate. The State of Nature is a context from which norms of right and wrong are excluded. The contrasting context, the State of Reason, implies an ethical foundation. In the State of Reason the distinction between what

is and what ought to be operates universally. The new context
can be constructed only by the inclusion of the standards and
norms that were defined as irrelevant to the description of the
State of Nature. Let it be assumed that the 'survival of the fit'
is a portion of this description. As such, the description may
include the fact that the good die young (assuming that this is
a fact); but the description does not in itself state whether the
fact ought, or ought not, obtain. It is, however, intellectually
necessary to raise this very question. When this is done, the
State of Nature is supplanted by the State of Reason. The life
of man, both as individual and as congregate, receives treatment
under a new system of ideas.

The analysis of society and the state, in other words, discloses the supreme functional validity of the distinction between
right and wrong, the true and the false. Analysis discloses a
principle of authority, and with this the conjoint subjection
of individual and group to the imperatives of Reason. As the
unity of congregate life in one context is the unity of the herd,
so within this new context the unity of the State is the unity
of the Life of Reason. The compact, therefore, rests upon the
omnipresence of reason within man. Society and the State are
grounded, not upon the biological fact that man possesses
powers as he has locomotion, but upon the fact that these
powers must acknowledge their own nature. The so-called
transfer of right implied in the contract can be a transfer only
because Reason recognizes the prerogatives of Reason. The
compact is a transformation in which animals become Citizens
and the herd becomes a Society. The equivalence of natural
right and power persists, but in a transfigured sense. Just as
civil right cannot mean right in the biological sense, so power
in the context of the Life of Reason cannot be identical with
power in the State of Nature. Civil Right indeed is natural,
but natural in that special sense to which Spinoza refers, for

it can be conceived only within the Life of Reason and within the State as the embodiment of Reason. Within the State of Nature, each man must act from the necessities of his own nature. What passion and desire may require, that a man does by natural right and by necessity. Intelligence properly furnishes guidance in the process of securing satisfaction of desire. This system of necessity defines Human Bondage. But when the intelligent animal becomes rationally awakened, when the authority of Reason is acknowledged, when its judicial functions are perceived, then man enters into a new bondage. The Bondage of Reason is Freedom. Within this new servitude that is freedom, however, man still acts from the necessities of his nature. As this nature is transfigured, so necessity is transfigured, Man, in the Life of Reason—or at least in so far as he pursues this life—acts from the necessities of a nature that is rationally ordered, intellectually enlightened, and possessed of freedom under the obligations of morality. And as the animal becomes a Citizen, so the herd becomes a Society: to act from necessity is to be subject to the necessities of Citizenship and of the State.

The kindliest of readers, who may charitably admit that some clarification is provided by this discussion of two contrasted universes of discourse, may nevertheless remain dissatisfied. However valid, for limited purposes, this separation of contexts may be, he will properly insist that somewhere the contrast must be resolved and a unity of doctrine be attained. The demand is just. Whether it can be provided within political philosophy itself is another question. With respect to the Spinozistic doctrine, at any rate, the answer must be in the negative. Spinoza's political teachings, with the intellectual implements involved, rest upon a metaphysical and theological basis. From the metaphysical basis the contextual contrast was developed.

The resolution of the contrast will require a return to meta-physics.

The reader may acknowledge this and still remain discontented. He will recall, perhaps, that Plato, having written the *Republic,* in later life wrote political dialogues described as less idealistic in purpose. The reader may wonder why a philosopher, having defined the State, should then consider states and discuss the defects and advantages of monarchy or aristocracy or democracy. He may wonder why Spinoza should ask what is the best state of a dominion. For, he may urge, the State is the State wherever it may be found and in whatever degree it may exist. The reader, however, must not be misled by this practice on the part of political philosophers. There are two questions involved in his task; the one is the definition of the State, and the complete development of what is implied in the definition. The other problem is that of determining the conditions within which the State may most fully come to be. For it is one thing, as Plato sufficiently has taught us, to define the State, and another thing to ensure that states shall be in actuality what the State indubitably is in idea. Spinoza has declared that dominion to be the best where men pass their lives in unity, and that such a life is defined above all by Reason. The Life of Reason is attained by few and by these only in a fragmentary way. For Spinoza the ideal at least is imperishable. In the language of the Improvement of the Understanding, the chief good for man is that he should arrive, together with other individuals if possible, at the "knowledge of the union existing between the mind and the whole of nature." For Spinoza here lies the solution of all problems for men in the State.

A. G. A. BALZ.

SELECTIONS

FROM THE

TRACTATUS THEOLOGICO-POLITICUS

A THEOLOGICO-POLITICAL TREATISE
CONTAINING CERTAIN DISCUSSIONS
WHEREIN IS SET FORTH THAT FREEDOM OF THOUGHT
AND SPEECH NOT ONLY MAY, WITHOUT PREJUDICE
TO PIETY AND THE PUBLIC PEACE, BE GRANTED;
BUT ALSO MAY NOT, WITHOUT DANGER
TO PIETY AND THE PUBLIC
PEACE, BE WITHHELD

"Hereby know we that we dwell in Him, and He in us, because He hath given us of His Spirit." 1 John iv. 13.

[A]

Preface

MEN would never be superstitious, if they could govern all their circumstances by set rules, or if they were always favoured by fortune: but being frequently driven into straits where rules are useless, and being often kept fluctuating pitiably between hope and fear by the uncertainty of fortune's greedily coveted favours, they are consequently, for the most part, very prone to credulity. The human mind is readily swerved this way or that in times of doubt, especially when hope and fear are struggling for the mastery, though usually it is boastful, over-confident, and vain.

This as a general fact I suppose everyone knows, though few, I believe, know their own nature; no one can have lived in the world without observing that most people, when in prosperity, are so over-brimming with wisdom (however inexperienced they may be), that they take every offer of advice as a personal insult, whereas in adversity they know not where to turn, but beg and pray for counsel from every passer-by. No plan is then too futile, too absurd, or too fatuous for their adoption; the most frivolous causes will raise them to hope, or plunge them into despair—if anything happens during their fright which reminds them of some past good or ill, they think it portends a happy or unhappy issue, and therefore (though it may have proved abortive a hundred times before) style it a lucky or unlucky omen. Anything which excites their astonishment they believe to be a portent signifying the anger of the gods or of the Supreme Being, and, mistaking superstition for religion, account it impious not to avert the evil with prayer and sacrifice. Signs and wonders of this sort they conjure up perpetually, till one might think Nature as mad as themselves, they interpret her so fantastically.

Thus it is brought prominently before us, that superstition's chief victims are those persons who greedily covet temporal advantages; they it is, who (especially when they are in danger, and cannot help themselves) are wont with prayers and woman-ish tears to implore help from God: upbraiding Reason as blind, because she cannot show a sure path to the shadows they pursue, and rejecting human wisdom as vain; but believing the phantoms of imagination, dreams, and other childish absurdities, to be the very oracles of Heaven. As though God had turned away from the wise, and written His decrees, not in the mind of man but in the entrails of beasts, or left them to be proclaimed by the inspiration and instinct of fools, madmen, and birds. Such is the unreason to which terror can drive mankind!

Superstition, then, is engendered, preserved, and fostered by fear. If anyone desire an example, let him take Alexander, who only began superstitiously to seek guidance from seers, when he first learnt to fear fortune in the passes of Sysis (Curtius, v. 4); whereas after he had conquered Darius he consulted prophets no more, till a second time frightened by reverses. When the Scythians were provoking a battle, the Bactrians had deserted, and he himself was lying sick of his wounds, "he once more turned to superstition, the mockery of human wisdom, and bade Aristander, to whom he confided his credulity, inquire the issue of affairs with sacrificed victims." Very numerous examples of a like nature might be cited, clearly showing the fact, that only while under the dominion of fear do men fall a prey to superstition; that all the portents ever invested with the reverence of misguided religion are mere phantoms of dejected and fearful minds; and lastly, that prophets have most power among the people, and are most formidable to rulers, precisely at those times when the state is in most peril. I think this is sufficiently plain to all, and will therefore say no more on the subject.

The origin of superstition above given affords us a clear reason for the fact, that it comes to all men naturally, though some refer its rise to a dim notion of God, universal to mankind, and also tends to show, that it is no less inconsistent and variable than other mental hallucinations and emotional impulses, and further that it can only be maintained by hope, hatred, anger, and deceit; since it springs, not from reason, but solely from the more powerful phases of emotion. Furthermore, we may readily understand how difficult it is, to maintain in the same course men prone to every form of credulity. For, as the mass of mankind remains always at about the same pitch of misery, it never assents long to any one remedy, but is always best pleased by a novelty which has not yet proved illusive.

This element of inconsistency has been the cause of many terrible wars and revolutions; for, as Curtius well says (lib. iv. chap. 10): "The mob has no ruler more potent than superstition," and is easily led, on the plea of religion, at one moment to adore its kings as gods, and anon to execrate and abjure them as humanity's common bane. Immense pains have therefore been taken to counteract this evil by investing religion, whether true or false, with such pomp and ceremony, that it may rise superior to every shock, and be always observed with studious reverence by the whole people—a system which has been brought to great perfection by the Turks, for they consider even controversy impious, and so clog men's minds with dogmatic formulas, that they leave no room for sound reason, not even enough to doubt with.

But if, in despotic statecraft, the supreme and essential mystery be to hoodwink the subjects, and to mask the fear, which keeps them down, with the specious garb of religion, so that men may fight as bravely for slavery as for safety, and count it not shame but highest honour to risk their blood and their lives for the vainglory of a tyrant; yet in a free state no more mischievous expedient could be planned or attempted. Wholly repugnant to the general freedom are such devices as enthralling men's minds with prejudices, forcing their judgment, or employing any of the weapons of quasi-religious sedition; indeed, such seditions only spring up, when law enters the domain of speculative thought, and opinions are put on trial and condemned on the same footing as crimes, while those who defend and follow them are sacrificed, not to public safety, but to their opponents' hatred and cruelty. If deeds only could be made the grounds of criminal charges, and words were always allowed to pass free, such seditions would be divested of every semblance of justification, and would be separated from mere controversies by a hard and fast line.

Now, seeing that we have the rare happiness of living in a republic, where everyone's judgment is free and unshackled, where each may worship God as his conscience dictates, and where freedom is esteemed before all things dear and precious, I have believed that I should be undertaking no ungrateful or unprofitable task, in demonstrating that not only can such freedom be granted without prejudice to the public peace, but also, that without such freedom, piety cannot flourish nor the public peace be secure.

Such is the chief conclusion I seek to establish in this treatise; but, in order to reach it, I must first point out the misconceptions which, like scars of our former bondage, still disfigure our notion of religion, and must expose the false views about the civil authority which many have most impudently advocated, endeavouring to turn the mind of the people, still prone to heathen superstition, away from its legitimate rulers, and so bring us again into slavery. As to the order of my treatise I will speak presently, but first I will recount the causes which led me to write.

I have often wondered, that persons who make a boast of professing the Christian religion, namely, love, joy, peace, temperance, and charity to all men, should quarrel with such rancorous animosity, and display daily towards one another such bitter hatred, that this, rather than the virtues they claim, is the readiest criterion of their faith. Matters have long since come to such a pass, that one can only pronounce a man Christian, Turk, Jew, or Heathen, by his general appearance and attire, by his frequenting this or that place of worship, or employing the phraseology of a particular sect—as for manner of life, it is in all cases the same. Inquiry into the cause of this anomaly leads me unhesitatingly to ascribe it to the fact, that the ministries of the Church are regarded by the masses merely as dignities, her offices as posts of emolument—in short, popular religion may be summed up as respect for ecclesiastics. The spread of this misconception inflamed every worthless fellow with an intense desire to enter holy orders, and thus the love of diffusing God's religion degenerated into sordid avarice and ambition. Every church became a theatre, where orators, instead of church teachers, harangued, caring not to instruct the people, but striving to attract admiration, to bring opponents to public scorn, and to preach only novelties and paradoxes, such as would tickle the ears of their congregation. This state of things necessarily stirred up an amount of controversy, envy, and hatred, which no lapse of time could appease; so that we can scarcely wonder that of the old religion nothing survives but its outward forms (even these, in the mouth of the multitude, seem rather adulation than adoration of the Deity), and that

faith has become a mere compound of credulity and prejudices
—aye, prejudices too, which degrade man from rational being
to beast, which completely stifle the power of judgment between true and false, which seem, in fact, carefully fostered for
the purpose of extinguishing the last spark of reason! Piety,
great God! and religion are become a tissue of ridiculous mysteries; men, who flatly despise reason, who reject and turn away
from understanding as naturally corrupt, these, I say, these of
all men, are thought, O lie most horrible! to possess light from
on High. Verily, if they had but one spark of light from on
High, they would not insolently rave, but would learn to worship God more wisely, and would be as marked among their
fellows for mercy as they now are for malice; if they were concerned for their opponents' souls, instead of for their own repu-
tations, they would no longer fiercely persecute, but rather be
filled with pity and compassion.

Furthermore, if any Divine light were in them, it would
appear from their doctrine. I grant that they are never tired of
professing their wonder at the profound mysteries of Holy
Writ; still I cannot discover that they teach anything but speculations of Platonists and Aristotelians, to which (in order to
save their credit for Christianity) they have made Holy Writ
conform; not content to rave with the Greeks themselves, they
want to make the prophets rave also; showing conclusively, that
never even in sleep have they caught a glimpse of Scripture's
Divine nature. The very vehemence of their admiration for the
mysteries plainly attests, that their belief in the Bible is a formal
assent rather than a living faith: and the fact is made still more
apparent by their laying down beforehand, as a foundation for
the study and true interpretation of Scripture, the principle that
it is in every passage true and divine. Such a doctrine should
be reached only after strict scrutiny and thorough comprehen-
sion of the Sacred Books (which would teach it much better,

for they stand in need of no human fictions), and not be set up on the threshold, as it were, of inquiry.

As I pondered over the facts that the light of reason is not only despised, but by many even execrated as a source of impiety, that human commentaries are accepted as divine records, and that credulity is extolled as faith; as I marked the fierce controversies of philosophers raging in Church and State, the source of bitter hatred and dissension, the ready instruments of sedition and other ills innumerable, I determined to examine the Bible afresh in a careful, impartial, and unfettered spirit, making no assumptions concerning it, and attributing to it no doctrines, which I do not find clearly therein set down. With these precautions I constructed a method of Scriptural interpretation, and thus equipped proceeded to inquire—What is prophecy? in what sense did God reveal Himself to the prophets, and why were these particular men chosen by Him? Was it on account of the sublimity of their thoughts about the Deity and nature, or was it solely on account of their piety? These questions being answered, I was easily able to conclude, that the authority of the prophets has weight only in matters of morality, and that their speculative doctrines affect us little.

Next I inquired, why the Hebrews were called God's chosen people, and discovering that it was only because God had chosen for them a certain strip of territory, where they might live peaceably and at ease, I learnt that the Law revealed by God to Moses was merely the law of the individual Hebrew state, therefore that it was binding on none but Hebrews, and not even on Hebrews after the downfall of their nation. Further, in order to ascertain, whether it could be concluded from Scripture, that the human understanding is naturally corrupt, I inquired whether the Universal Religion, the Divine Law revealed through the Prophets and Apostles to the whole human race, differs from that which is taught by the light of natural reason, whether miracles can take place in violation of the laws of nature, and if so, whether they imply the existence of God more surely and clearly than events, which we understand plainly and distinctly through their immediate natural causes.

Now, as in the whole course of my investigation I found nothing taught expressly by Scripture, which does not agree with our understanding, or which is repugnant thereto, and as I saw that the prophets taught nothing, which is not very simple and easily to be grasped by all, and further, that they clothed their teaching in the style, and confirmed it with the reasons, which would most deeply move the mind of the masses to devotion towards God, I became thoroughly convinced, that the Bible leaves reason absolutely free, that it has nothing in common with philosophy, in fact, that Revelation and Philosophy stand on totally different footings. In order to set this forth categorically and exhaust the whole question, I point out the way in which the Bible should be interpreted, and show that all knowledge of spiritual questions should be sought from it alone, and not from the objects of ordinary knowledge. Thence I pass on to indicate the false notions, which have arisen from the fact that the multitude—ever prone to super-stition, and caring more for the shreds of antiquity than for eternal truths—pays homage to the Books of the Bible, rather than to the Word of God. I show that the Word of God has not been revealed as a certain number of books, but was dis-played to the prophets as a simple idea of the Divine mind, namely, obedience to God in singleness of heart, and in the practice of justice and charity; and I further point out, that this doctrine is set forth in Scripture in accordance with the opinions and understandings of those, among whom the Apos-tles and Prophets preached, to the end that men might receive it willingly, and with their whole heart.

Having thus laid bare the bases of belief, I draw the conclusion that Revelation has obedience for its sole object, and therefore, in purpose no less than in foundation and method, stands entirely aloof from ordinary knowledge; each has its separate province, neither can be called the handmaid of the other.

Furthermore, as men's habits of mind differ, so that some more readily embrace one form of faith, some another, for what moves one to pray may move another only to scoff, I conclude, in accordance with what has gone before, that everyone should be free to choose for himself the foundations of his creed, and that faith should be judged only by its fruits; each would then obey God freely with his whole heart, while nothing would be publicly honoured save justice and charity.

Having thus drawn attention to the liberty conceded to everyone by the revealed law of God, I pass on to another part of my subject, and prove that this same liberty can and should be accorded with safety to the state and the magisterial authority —in fact, that it cannot be withheld without great danger to peace and detriment to the community.

In order to establish my point, I start from the natural rights of the individual, which are co extensive with his desires and power, and from the fact that no one is bound to live as another pleases, but is the guardian of his own liberty. I show that these rights can only be transferred to those whom we depute to defend us, who acquire with the duties of defence the power of ordering our lives, and I thence infer that rulers possess rights only limited by their power, that they are the sole guardians of justice and liberty, and that their subjects should act in all things as they dictate: nevertheless, since no one can so utterly abdicate his own power of self-defence as to cease to be a man, I conclude that no one can be deprived of his natural rights absolutely, but that subjects, either by tacit agreement, or by social contract, retain a certain number, which cannot be taken from them without great danger to the state.

From these considerations I pass on to the Hebrew State, which I describe at some length, in order to trace the manner in which Religion acquired the force of law, and to touch on other noteworthy points. I then prove, that the holders of sovereign power are the depositaries and interpreters of religious no less than of civil ordinances, and that they alone have the right to decide what is just or unjust, pious or impious; lastly, I conclude by showing, that they best retain this right and secure safety to their state by allowing every man to think what he likes, and say what he thinks.

Such, Philosophical Reader, are the questions I submit to your notice, counting on your approval, for the subject matter of the whole book and of the several chapters is important, profitable. I would say more, but I do not want my preface to extend to a volume, especially as I know that its leading propositions are to Philosophers but commonplaces. To the rest of mankind I care not to commend my treatise, for I cannot expect that it contains anything to please them: I know how deeply rooted are the prejudices embraced under the name of religion; I am aware that in the mind of the masses superstition is no less deeply rooted than fear; I recognize that their constancy is here obstinacy, and that they are led to praise or blame by impulse rather than reason. Therefore the multitude, and those of like passions with the multitude, I ask not to read my book; nay, I would rather that they should utterly neglect it, than that they should misinterpret it after their wont. They would gain no good themselves, and might prove a stumbling-block to others, whose philosophy is hampered by the belief that Reason is a mere handmaid to Theology, and whom I seek in this work especially to benefit. But as there will be many who have neither the leisure, nor, perhaps, the inclination to read through all I have written, I feel bound here, as at the end of my treatise, to declare that I have written nothing, which I do not most willingly submit to the examination and judgment of my country's rulers, and that I am ready to retract anything, which they shall decide to be repugnant to the laws or prejudicial to the public good. I know that I am a man and, as a man, liable to error, but against error I have taken scrupulous care, and striven to keep in entire accordance with the laws of my country, with loyalty, and with morality.[1]

[1] Spinoza's position will be clarified for the reader by consideration of the following paragraphs taken from Chapter XIV (not re-printed in the present volume). Chapter XIV has the following title: "Definitions of Faith, the True Faith, and the Foundations of Faith, which is once for all separated from Philosophy." In this chapter we are told that "to separate faith from philosophy" is the "chief aim of the whole Treatise." The nature of Faith and Spinoza's notion of the content of the Universal Religion are conveyed in the following paragraphs:

"Faith consists in a knowledge of God, without which obedience to Him would be impossible, and which the mere fact of obedience to Him implies. This definition is so clear, and follows so plainly from what we have already proved, that it needs no explanation. The consequences involved therein I will now briefly show. (I.) Faith is not salutary in itself, but only in respect to the obedience it implies, or as James puts it in his Epistle, ii. 17, 'Faith without works is dead' (see the whole of the chapter quoted). (II.) He who is truly obedient necessarily possesses true and saving faith; for if obedience be granted, faith must be granted also, as the same Apostle expressly says in these words (ii. 18), 'Show me thy faith without thy works, and I will show thee my faith by my works.' So also John, 1 Ep. iv. 7: 'Everyone that loveth is born of God, and knoweth God: he that loveth not, knoweth not God; for God is love.' From these texts, I repeat, it follows that we can only judge a man faithful or unfaithful by his works. If his works be good, he is faithful, however much his doctrines may differ from those of the rest of the faithful: if his works be evil, though he may verbally conform, he is unfaithful. For obedience implies faith, and faith without works is dead."

"Lastly, it follows that faith does not demand that dogmas should be true as that they should be pious—that is, such as will stir up the heart to obey; though there be many such which contain not a shadow of truth, so long as they be held in good faith, otherwise their adherents are disobedient, for how can anyone, desirous of loving justice and obeying God, adore as Divine what he knows to be alien from the Divine nature? However, men may err from simplicity of mind, and Scripture, as we have seen, does not condemn ignorance, but obstinacy. This is the necessary result of our definition of faith, and all its branches should spring from the universal rule above given, and from the evident aim and object of the Bible, unless we choose to mix our own inventions therewith. Thus it is not true doctrines which are expressly required by the Bible, so much as doctrines necessary for obedience, and to confirm in our hearts the love of our neighbour, wherein (to adopt the words of John) we are in God, and God in us.

"As, then, each man's faith must be judged pious or impious only in respect of its producing obedience or obstinacy, and not in respect of its truth; and as no one will dispute that men's dispositions are exceedingly varied, that all do not acquiesce in the same things, but are ruled some by one opinion some by another, so that what moves one to devotion moves another to laughter and contempt, it follows that there can be no doctrines in the Catholic, or universal, religion, which can give rise to controversy among good men. Such doctrines might be pious to some and impious to others, whereas they should be judged solely by their fruits.

"To the universal religion, then, belong only such dogmas as are absolutely required in order to attain obedience to God, and without which such obedience would be impossible; as for the rest, each man—seeing that he is the best judge of his own character—should adopt whatever he thinks best adapted to strengthen his love of justice. If this were so, I think there would be no further occasion for controversies in the Church.

"I have now no further fear in enumerating the dogmas of universal faith or the fundamental dogmas of the whole of Scripture, inasmuch as they all tend (as may be seen from what has been said) to this one doctrine, namely, that there exists a God, that is, a Supreme Being, Who loves justice and charity, and Who must be obeyed by whosoever would be saved; that the worship of this Being consists in the practice of justice and love towards one's neighbour, and that they contain nothing beyond the following doctrines:—

"I. That God or a Supreme Being exists, sovereignly just and merciful, the Exemplar of the true life; that whosoever is ignorant of or disbelieves in His existence cannot obey Him or know Him as a Judge.

"II. That He is One. Nobody will dispute that this doctrine is absolutely necessary for entire devotion, admiration, and love towards God. For devotion, admiration, and love spring from the superiority of one over all else.

"III. That He is omnipresent, or that all things are open to Him, for if anything could be supposed to be concealed from Him, or to be unnoticed by Him, we might doubt or be ignorant of the equity of His judgment as directing all things.

"IV. That He has supreme right and dominion over all things, and that

He does nothing under compulsion, but by His absolute fiat and grace. All things are bound to obey Him, He is not bound to obey any.

"V. That the worship of God consists only in justice and charity, or love towards one's neighbour.

"VI. That all those, and those only, who obey God by their manner of life are saved; the rest of mankind, who live under the sway of their pleasures, are lost. If we did not believe this, there would be no reason for obeying God rather than pleasure.

"VII. Lastly, that God forgives the sins of those who repent. No one is free from sin, so that without this belief all would despair of salvation, and there would be no reason for believing in the mercy of God. He who firmly believes that God, out of the mercy and grace with which He directs all things, forgives the sins of men, and who feels his love of God kindled thereby, he, I say, does really know Christ according to the Spirit, and Christ is in him.

"No one can deny that all these doctrines are before all things necessary to be believed, in order that every man, without exception, may be able to obey God according to the bidding of the Law above explained, for if one of these precepts be disregarded obedience is destroyed. But as to what God, or the Exemplar of the true life, may be, whether fire, or spirit, or light, or thought, or what not, this, I say, has nothing to do with faith any more than has the question how He comes to be the Exemplar of the true life, whether it be because He has a just and merciful mind, or because all things exist and act through Him, and consequently that we understand through Him, and through Him see what is truly just and good. Everyone may think on such questions as he likes.

"Furthermore, faith is not affected, whether we hold that God is omnipresent essentially or potentially; that He directs all things by absolute fiat, or by the necessity of His nature; that He dictates laws like a prince, or that He sets them forth as eternal truths; that man obeys Him by virtue of free will, or by virtue of the necessity of the Divine decree; lastly, that the reward of the good and the punishment of the wicked is natural or supernatural: these and such like questions have no bearing on faith, except in so far as they are used as means to give us license to sin more, or to obey God less. I will go further, and maintain that every man is bound to adapt these dogmas to his own way of thinking, and to interpret them according as he feels that he can give them his fullest and most unhesitating assent, so that he may the more easily obey God with his whole heart.

"Such was the manner, as we have already pointed out, in which the faith was in old time revealed and written, in accordance with the understanding and opinions of the prophets and people of the period; so, in like fashion, every man is bound to adapt it to his own opinions, so that he may accept it without any hesitation or mental repugnance. We have shown that faith does not so much require truth as piety, and that it is only quickening and pious through obedience, consequently no one is faithful save by obedience alone. The best faith is not necessarily possessed by him who displays the best reasons, but by him who displays the best fruits of justice and charity. How salutary and necessary this doctrine is for a state, in order that men may dwell together in peace and concord; and how many and how great causes of disturbance and crime are thereby cut off, I leave everyone to judge for himself!"

"It remains for me to show that between faith or theology, and philosophy, there is no connection, nor affinity. I think no one will dispute the fact who has knowledge of the aim and foundations of the two subjects, for they are as wide apart as the poles.

"Philosophy has no end in view save truth: faith, as we have abundantly proved, looks for nothing but obedience and piety. Again, philosophy is based on axioms which must be sought from nature alone: faith is based on history and language, and must be sought for only in Scripture and revelation, as we showed in Chap. VII. Faith, therefore, allows the greatest latitude in philosophic speculation, allowing us without blame to think what we like about anything, and only condemning, as heretics and schismatics, those who teach opinions which tend to produce obstinacy, hatred, strife, and anger; while, on the other hand, only considering as faithful those who persuade us, as far as their reason and faculties will permit, to follow justice and charity."

Chapter IV

Of the Divine Law

[In part]

THE word law, taken in the abstract (*absolute*), means that by which an individual, or all things, or as many things as belong to a particular species, act in one and the same fixed and definite manner, which manner depends either on natural necessity or on human decree. A law (*lex*) which depends on natural necessity is one which necessarily follows from the nature, or from the definition of the thing in question; a law which depends on human decree, and which is more correctly called an ordinance (*jus*), is one which men have laid down for themselves and others in order to live more safely or conveniently, or from some similar reason.

For example, the law that all bodies impinging on lesser bodies, lose as much of their own motion as they communicate to the latter is a universal law of all bodies, and depends on natural necessity. So, too, the law that a man in remembering one thing, straightway remembers another either like it, or which he had perceived simultaneously with it, is a law which neecssarily follows from the nature of man. But the law that men must yield, or be compelled to yield, somewhat of their natural right, and that they bind themselves to live in a certain way, depends on human decree. Now, though I freely admit that all things are predetermined by universal natural laws to exist and operate in a given, fixed, and definite manner, I still assert that the laws I have just mentioned depend on human decree.

(1.) Because man, in so far as he is a part of nature, constitutes a part of the power of nature. Whatever, therefore, follows necessarily from the necessity of human nature (that is, from nature herself, in so far as we conceive of her as acting through man) follows, even though it be necessarily, from human power. Hence the sanction of such laws may very well be said to depend on man's decree, for it principally depends on the power of the human mind; so that the human mind in respect to its perception of things as true and false, can readily be conceived as without such laws, but not without necessary law as we have just defined it.

(2.) I have stated that these laws depend on human decree because it is well to define and explain things by their proximate causes. The general consideration of fate and the concatenation of causes would aid us very little in forming and arranging our ideas concerning particular questions. Let us add that as to the actual co-ordination and concatenation of things, that is how things are ordained and linked together, we are obviously ignorant; therefore, it is more profitable for right living, nay, it is necessary for us to consider things as contingent. So much about law in the abstract.

Now the word law seems to be only applied to natural phenomena by analogy, and is commonly taken to signify a command which men can either obey or neglect, inasmuch as it restrains human nature within certain originally exceeded limits, and therefore lays down no rule beyond human strength. Thus it is expedient to define law more particularly as a plan of life laid down by man for himself or others with a certain purpose.

However, as the true object of legislation is only perceived by a few, and most men are almost incapable of grasping it, though they live under its conditions, legislators, with a view to exacting general obedience, have wisely put forward another object, very different from that which necessarily follows from the nature of law: they promise to the observers of the law that which the masses chiefly desire, and threaten its violators with that which they chiefly fear: thus endeavouring to restrain the masses, as far as may be, like a horse with a curb; whence it follows that the word law is chiefly applied to the modes of life enjoined on men by the sway of others; hence those who obey the law are said to live under it and to be under compulsion. In truth, a man who renders everyone their due because he fears the gallows, acts under the sway and compulsion of others, and cannot be called just. But a man who does the same from a knowledge of the true reason for laws and their necessity, acts from a firm purpose and of his own accord, and is therefore properly called just. This, I take it, is Paul's meaning when he says, that those who live under the law cannot be justified through the law, for justice, as commonly defined, is the constant and perpetual will to render every man his due. Thus Solomon says (Prov. xxi. 15), "It is a joy to the just to do judgment," but the wicked fear.

Law, then, being a plan (*ratio*) of living which men have for a certain object laid down for themselves or others, may, as it seems, be divided into human law and Divine law.

By human law I mean a plan of living which serves only to render life and the state secure.

By Divine law I mean that which only regards the highest good, in other words, the true knowledge of God and love.

I call this law Divine because of the nature of the highest good, which I will here shortly explain as clearly as I can.

Inasmuch as the intellect is the best part of our being, it

is evident that we should make every effort to perfect it as far as possible if we desire to search for what is really profitable to us. For in intellectual perfection the highest good should consist. Now, since all our knowledge, and the certainty which removes every doubt, depend solely on the knowledge of God;—firstly, because without God nothing can exist or be conceived; secondly, because so long as we have no clear and distinct idea of God we may remain in universal doubt—it follows that our highest good and perfection also depend solely on the knowledge of God. Further, since without God nothing can exist or be conceived, it is evident that all natural phenomena involve and express the conception of God as far as their essence and perfection extend, so that we have greater and more perfect knowledge of God in proportion to our knowledge of natural phenomena: for (since the knowledge of an effect through its cause is the same thing as the knowledge of a particular property of a cause) the greater our knowledge of natural phenomena, the more perfect is our knowledge of the essence of God (which is the cause of all things). So, then, our highest good not only depends on the knowledge of God, but wholly consists therein; and it further follows that man is perfect or the reverse in proportion to the nature and perfection of the object of his special desire; hence the most perfect and the chief sharer in the highest blessedness is he who prizes above all else, and takes especial delight in, the intellectual knowledge of God, the most perfect Being.

Hither, then, our highest good and our highest blessedness aim—namely, to the knowledge and love of God; therefore the means demanded by this aim of all human actions, that is, by God in so far as the idea of Him is in us, may be called the commands of God, because they proceed, as it were, from God Himself, inasmuch as He exists in our minds, and the

plan of life which has regard to this aim may be fitly called
the law of God.

The nature of the means, and the plan of life which this
aim demands, how the foundations of the best states follow
its lines, and how men's life is conducted, are questions pertaining to general ethics. Here I only proceed to treat of the
Divine law in a particular application.

As the love of God is man's highest happiness and blessedness, and the ultimate end and aim of all human actions, it
follows that he alone lives by the Divine law who loves God
not from fear of punishment, or from love of any other object, such as sensual pleasure, fame, or the like; but solely
because he has knowledge of God, or is convinced that the
knowledge and love of God is the highest good. The sum
and chief precept, then, of the Divine law is to love God as
the highest good, namely, as we have said, not from fear of
any pains and penalties, or from the love of any other object
in which we desire to take pleasure. The idea of God lays
down the rule that God is our highest good—in other words,
that the knowledge and love of God is the ultimate aim to
which all our actions should be directed. The worldling cannot understand these things, they appear foolishness to him,
because he has too meagre a knowledge of God, and also because in this highest good he can discover nothing which he
can handle or eat, or which affects the fleshly appetites wherein
he chiefly delights, for it consists solely in thought and the
pure reason. They, on the other hand, who know that they
possess no greater gift than intellect and sound reason, will
doubtless accept what I have said without question.

We have now explained that wherein the Divine law chiefly
consists, and what are human laws, namely, all those which
have a different aim unless they have been ratified by revelation, for in this respect also things are referred to God (as

we have shown above) and in this sense the law of Moses, although it was not universal, but entirely adapted to the disposition and particular preservation of a single people, may yet be called a law of God or Divine law, inasmuch as we believe that it was ratified by prophetic insight. If we consider the nature of natural Divine law as we have just explained it, we shall see

I. That it is universal or common to all men, for we have deduced it from universal human nature.

II. That it does not depend on the truth of any historical narrative whatsoever, for inasmuch as this natural Divine law is comprehended solely by the consideration of human nature, it is plain that we can conceive it as existing as well in Adam as in any other man, as well in a man living among his fellows, as in a man who lives by himself.

The truth of a historical narrative, however assured, cannot give us the knowledge nor consequently the love of God, for love of God springs from knowledge of Him, and knowledge of Him should be derived from general ideas, in themselves certain and known, so that the truth of a historical narrative is very far from being a necessary requisite for our attaining our highest good.

Still, though the truth of histories cannot give us the knowledge and love of God, I do not deny that reading them is very useful with a view to life in the world, for the more we have observed and known of men's customs and circumstances, which are best revealed by their actions, the more warily we shall be able to order our lives among them, and so far as reason dictates to adapt our actions to their dispositions.

III. We see that this natural Divine law does not demand the performance of ceremonies—that is, actions in themselves indifferent, which are called good from the fact of their institution, or actions symbolizing something profitable for salvation, or (if one prefers this definition) actions of which the meaning surpasses human understanding. The natural light of reason does not demand anything which it is itself unable to supply, but only such as it can very clearly show to be good, or a means to our blessedness. Such things as are good simply because they have been commanded or instituted, or as being symbols of something good, are mere shadows which cannot be reckoned among actions that are the offspring, as it were, or fruit of a sound mind and of intellect. There is no need for me to go into this now in more detail.

IV. Lastly, we see that the highest reward of the Divine law is the law itself, namely, to know God and to love Him of our free choice, and with an undivided and fruitful spirit; while its penalty is the absence of these things, and being in bondage to the flesh—that is, having an inconstant and wavering spirit.

CHAPTER V

OF THE CEREMONIAL LAW

[In part]

THE formation of society serves not only for defensive purposes, but is also very useful, and, indeed, absolutely
necessary, as rendering possible the division of labour. If men
did not render mutual assistance to each other, no one would
have either the skill or the time to provide for his own sus-
tenance and preservation: for all men are not equally apt for
all work, and no one would be capable of preparing all that
he individually stood in need of. Strength and time, I repeat,
would fail, if every one had in person to plough, to sow, to
reap, to grind corn, to cook, to weave, to stitch, and perform
the other numerous functions required to keep life going; to
say nothing of the arts and sciences which are also entirely
necessary to the perfection and blessedness of human nature.
We see that peoples living in uncivilized barbarism lead a
wretched and almost animal life, and even they would not be
able to acquire their few rude necessaries without assisting one
another to a certain extent.

Now if men were so constituted by nature that they desired nothing but what is designated by true reason, society
would obviously have no need of laws: it would be sufficient to
inculcate true moral doctrines; and men would freely, without hesitation, act in accordance with their true interests. But

24

human nature is framed in a different fashion: every one, indeed, seeks his own interest, but does not do so in accordance with the dictates of sound reason, for most men's ideas of desirability and usefulness are guided by their fleshly instincts and emotions, which take no thought beyond the present and the immediate object. Therefore, no society can exist without government, and force, and laws to restrain and repress men's desires and immoderate impulses. Still human nature will not submit to absolute repression. Violent governments, as Seneca says, never last long; the moderate governments endure.

So long as men act simply from fear they act contrary to their inclinations, taking no thought for the advantages or necessity of their actions, but simply endeavouring to escape punishment or loss of life. They must needs rejoice in any evil which befalls their ruler, even if it should involve themselves; and must long for and bring about such evil by every means in their power. Again, men are especially intolerant of serving and being ruled by their equals. Lastly, it is exceedingly difficult to revoke liberties once granted.

From these considerations it follows, firstly, that authority (*imperium*) should either be vested in the hands of the whole state in common, so that everyone should be bound to serve, and yet not be in subjection to his equals; or else, if power be in the hands of a few, or one man, that one man should be something above average humanity, or should strive to get himself accepted as such. Secondly, laws should in every government be so arranged that people should be kept in bounds by the hope of some greatly-desired good, rather than by fear, for then everyone will do his duty willingly.

Lastly, as obedience consists in acting at the bidding of external authority, it would have no place in a state where the government is vested in the whole people, and where laws are made by common consent. In such a society the people would remain free, whether the laws were added to or diminished, inasmuch as it would not be done on external authority, but their own free consent. The reverse happens when the sovereign power is vested in one man, for all act at his bidding; and, therefore, unless they had been trained from the first to depend on the words of their ruler, the latter would find it difficult, in case of need, to abrogate liberties once conceded, and impose new laws.

Chapter XVI

Of the Foundations of a State; of the Natural and Civil Rights of Individuals; and of the Rights of the Sovereign Power

HITHERTO our care has been to separate philosophy from theology, and to show the freedom of thought which such separation insures to both. It is now time to determine the limits to which such freedom of thought and discussion may extend itself in the ideal state (*Respublica*). For the due consideration of this question we must examine the foundations of a state, first turning our attention to the natural rights of individuals, and afterwards to religion and the state as a whole.

By the right and ordinance of nature, I merely mean those natural laws of every individual wherewith we conceive every individual to be conditioned by nature, so as to live and act in a given way. For instance, fishes are naturally conditioned for swimming, and the greater for devouring the less; therefore fishes enjoy the water, and the greater devour the less by sovereign natural right. For it is certain that nature, considered absolutely, has sovereign right to do anything she can; in other words, her right is co-extensive with her power. The power of nature is the power of God, which has sovereign right over all things; and, inasmuch as the universal power of nature is simply the aggregate of the powers of all her individual components, it follows that every individual has sovereign right to do all that he can; in other words, the rights of an individual extend to the utmost limits of his power as it has been conditioned. Now it is the sovereign law and right of nature that each individual should endeavour to preserve itself as it is, without regard to anything but itself; therefore this sovereign law and right belongs to every individual, namely, to exist and act according to its natural conditions. We do not here acknowledge any difference between mankind and other individual natural entities, nor between men endowed with reason and those to whom reason is unknown; nor between fools, madmen, and sane men. Whatsoever an individual does by the laws of its nature it has a sovereign right to do, inasmuch as it acts as it was conditioned by nature, and cannot act otherwise. Wherefore among men, so long as they are considered as living under the sway of nature, he who does not yet know reason, or who has not yet acquired the habit of virtue, acts solely according to the laws of his desire with as sovereign a right as he who orders his life entirely by the laws of reason.

That is, as the wise man has sovereign right to do all that reason dictates, or to live according to the laws of reason, so also the ignorant and foolish man has sovereign right to do all that desire dictates, or to live according to the laws of desire. This is identical with the teaching of Paul, who acknowledges that previous to the law—that is, so long as men are considered of as living under the sway of nature,—there is no sin.

The natural right of the individual man is thus determined, not by sound reason, but by desire and power. All are not naturally conditioned so as to act according to the laws and rules of reason; nay, on the contrary, all men are born ignorant, and before they can learn the right way of life and acquire the habit of virtue, the greater part of their life, even if they have been well brought up, has passed away. Nevertheless, they are in the meanwhile bound to live and preserve themselves as far as they can by the unaided impulses of desire. Nature has given them no other guide, and has denied them the present power of living according to sound reason; so that they are no more bound to live by the dictates of an enlightened mind, than a cat is bound to live by the laws of the nature of a lion.

Whatsoever, therefore, an individual (considered as under the sway [*imperium*] of nature) thinks useful for himself, whether led by sound reason or impelled by the passions, that he has a sovereign right to seek and to take for himself as he best can, whether by force, cunning, entreaty, or any other means; consequently he may regard as an enemy anyone who hinders the accomplishment of his purpose.

It follows from what we have said that the right and ordinance of nature, under which all men are born, and under which they mostly live, only prohibits such things as no one desires, and no one can attain: it does not forbid strife, nor hatred, nor anger, nor deceit, nor, indeed, any of the means suggested by desire.

This we need not wonder at, for nature is not bounded by the laws of human reason, which aims only at man's true benefit and preservation; her limits are infinitely wider, and have reference to the eternal order of nature, wherein man is but a speck; it is by the necessity of this alone that all individuals are conditioned for living and acting in a particular way. If anything, therefore, in nature seems to us ridiculous, absurd, or evil, it is because we only know in part, and are almost entirely ignorant of the order and interdependence of nature as a whole, and also because we want everything to be arranged according to the dictates of our human reason; in reality that which reason considers evil, is not evil in respect to the order and laws of nature as a whole, but only in respect to the laws of our reason.

Nevertheless, no one can doubt that it is much better for us to live according to the laws and assured dictates of reason, for, as we said, they have men's true good for their object. Moreover, everyone wishes to live as far as possible securely beyond the reach of fear, and this would be quite impossible so long as everyone did everything he liked, and reason's claim was lowered to a par with those of hatred and anger; there is no one who is not ill at ease in the midst of enmity, hatred, anger, and deceit, and who does not seek to avoid them as much as he can. When we reflect that men without mutual help, or the aid of reason, must needs live most miserably, as we clearly proved in Chap. V., we shall plainly see that men must necessarily come to an agreement to live together as securely and well as possible if they are to enjoy as a whole the rights which naturally belong to them as individuals, and their life should be no more conditioned by the force and desire of individuals, but by the power and will of the whole body. This end they will be unable to attain if desire be their only guide (for by the laws of desire each man is drawn in a different direction); they must, therefore, most firmly decree and establish that they will be guided in everything by reason (which nobody will dare openly to repudiate lest he should be taken for a madman), and will restrain any desire which is injurious to a man's fellows, that they will do to all as they would be done by, and that they will defend their neighbour's rights as their own.

How such a compact as this should be entered into, how ratified and established, we will now inquire.

Now it is a universal law of human nature that no one ever neglects anything which he judges to be good, except with the hope of gaining a greater good, or from the fear of a greater evil; nor does anyone endure an evil except for the sake of avoiding a greater evil, or gaining a greater good. That is, everyone will, of two goods, choose that which he thinks the greater; and, of two evils, that which he thinks the lesser. I say advisedly that which he thinks the greater or the lesser, for it does not necessarily follow that he judges right. This law is so deeply implanted in the human mind that it ought to be counted among eternal truths and axioms.

As a necessary consequence of the principle just enunciated, no one can honestly promise to forego the right which he has over all things,[1] and in general no one will abide by his promises, unless under the fear of a greater evil, or the hope of a greater good. An example will make the matter clearer. Suppose that a robber forces me to promise that I will give him my goods at his will and pleasure. It is plain (inasmuch as my natural right is, as I have shown, co-extensive with my power) that if I can free myself from this robber by stratagem, by assenting to his demands, I have the natural right to do so, and to pretend to accept his conditions. Or again, suppose I have genuinely promised someone that for the space of twenty days I will not taste food or any nourishment; and suppose I afterwards find that my promise was foolish, and cannot be kept without very great injury to myself; as I am bound by natural law and right to choose the lesser of two evils, I have complete right to break my compact, and act as if my promise had never been uttered. I say that I should have perfect natural right to do so, whether I was actuated by true and evident reason, or whether I was actuated by mere opinion in thinking I had promised rashly; whether my reasons were true or false, I should be in fear of a greater evil, which, by the ordinance of nature, I should strive to avoid by every means in my power.

[1] See author's note 1, p. 74.

We may, therefore, conclude that a compact is only made valid by its utility, without which it becomes null and void. It is, therefore, foolish to ask a man to keep his faith with us for ever, unless we also endeavour that the violation of the compact we enter into shall involve for the violator more harm than good. This consideration should have very great weight in forming a state. However, if all men could be easily led by reason alone, and could recognize what is best and most useful for a state, there would be no one who would not forswear deceit, for everyone would keep most religiously to their compact in their desire for the chief good, namely, the preservation of the state, and would cherish good faith above all things as the shield and buckler of the commonwealth. However, it is far from being the case that all men can always be easily led by reason alone; everyone is drawn away by his pleasure, while avarice, ambition, envy, hatred, and the like so engross the mind that reason has no place therein. Hence, though men make promises with all the appearances of good faith, and agree that they will keep to their engagement, no one can absolutely rely on another man's promise unless there is something behind it. Everyone has by nature a right to act deceitfully, and to break his compacts, unless he be restrained by the hope of some greater good, or the fear of some greater evil.

However, as we have shown that the natural right of the individual is only limited by his power, it is clear that by transferring, either willingly or under compulsion, this power into the hands of another, he in so doing necessarily cedes also a part of his right; and further, that the sovereign right over all men belongs to him who has sovereign power, wherewith he can compel men by force, or restrain them by threats of the universally feared punishment of death; such sovereign right he will retain only so long as he can maintain his power of enforcing his will; otherwise he will totter on his throne, and no one who is stronger than he will be bound unwillingly to obey him.

In this manner a society (*Societas*) can be formed without any violation of natural right, and the covenant can always be strictly kept—that is, if each individual hands over the whole of his power to the body politic (*Societas*), the latter will then possess sovereign natural right over all things; that is, it will have sole and unquestioned dominion, and everyone will be bound to obey, under pain of the severest punishment. A body politic of this kind is called a Democracy, which may be defined as a society which wields all its power as a whole.[2] The sovereign power is not restrained by any laws, but everyone is bound to obey it in all things; such is the state of things implied when men either tacitly or expressly handed over to it all their power of self-defence, or in other words, all their right. For if they had wished to retain any right for themselves, they ought to have taken precautions for its defence and preservation; as they have not done so, and indeed could not have done so without dividing and consequently ruining the state, they placed themselves absolutely at the mercy of the sovereign power; and, therefore, having acted (as we have shown) as reason and necessity demanded, they are obliged to fulfil the commands of the sovereign power, however absurd these may be, else they will be public enemies, and will act against reason, which urges the preservation of the state as a primary duty. For reason bids us choose the lesser of two evils.

Furthermore, this danger of submitting absolutely to the dominion and will of another, is one which may be incurred with a light heart; for we have shown that sovereigns only possess this right of imposing their will, so long as they have

---

[2] "Talis vero societatis jus Democratia vocatur, quae proinde definitur cœtus universus hominum, qui collegialiter summum jus ad omnia, quæ potest, habet."

the full power to enforce it: if such power be lost their right to command is lost also, or lapses to those who have assumed it and can keep it. Thus it is very rare for sovereigns to impose thoroughly irrational commands, for they are bound to consult their own interests, and retain their power by consulting the public good and acting according to the dictates of reason, as Seneca says, *"violenta imperia nemo continuit diu."* No one can long retain a tyrant's sway.

In a democracy, irrational commands are still less to be feared: for it is almost impossible that the majority of a people, especially if it be a large one, should agree in an irrational design: and, moreover, the basis and aim of a democracy is to avoid the desires as irrational, and to bring men as far as possible under the control of reason, so that they may live in peace and harmony: if this basis be removed the whole fabric falls to ruin.

Such being the ends in view for the sovereign power, the duty of subjects is, as I have said, to obey its commands, and to recognize no right save that which it sanctions.

It will, perhaps, be thought that we are turning subjects into slaves: for slaves obey commands and free men live as they like; but this idea is based on a misconception, for the true slave is he who is led away by his pleasures and can neither see what is good for him nor act accordingly: he alone is free who lives with free consent under the entire guidance of reason.

Action in obedience to orders does take away freedom in a certain sense, but it does not, therefore, make a man a slave, all depends on the object of the action. If the object of the action be the good of the state, and not the good of the agent, the latter is a slave and does himself no good: but in a Commonwealth and Dominion (*in Republica et Imperio*) where the weal of the whole people, and not that of the ruler, is the supreme law, obedience to the sovereign power does not make a man a slave, of no use to himself, but a subject. Therefore, that state is the freest whose laws are founded on sound reason, so that every member of it may, if he will, be free;[3] that is, live with full consent under the entire guidance of reason.

Children, though they are bound to obey all the commands of their parents, are yet not slaves: for the commands of parents look generally to the children's benefit.

We must, therefore, acknowledge a great difference between a slave, a son, and a subject; their positions may be thus defined. A slave is one who is bound to obey his master's orders, though they are given solely in the master's interest: a son is one who obeys his father's orders, given in his own interest; a subject obeys the orders of the sovereign power, given for the common interest, wherein he is included.

I think I have now shown sufficiently clearly the basis of a democracy: I have especially desired to do so, for I believe it to be of all forms of government the most natural, and the most consonant with individual liberty. In it no one transfers his natural right so absolutely that he has no further voice in affairs, he only hands it over to the majority of a society, whereof he is a unit. Thus all men remain, as they were in the state of nature, equals.

This is the only form of government which I have treated of at length, for it is the one most akin to my purpose of showing the benefits of freedom in a state.

I may pass over the fundamental principles of other forms of government, for we may gather from what has been said whence their right arises without going into its origin. The possessor of sovereign power, whether he be one, or many, or the whole body politic, has the sovereign right of imposing any commands he pleases: and he who has either voluntarily,

[3] See author's note 2, p. 74.

or under compulsion, transferred the right to defend him to another, has, in so doing, renounced his natural right and is therefore bound to obey, in all things, the commands of the sovereign power; and will be bound so to do so long as the king, or nobles, or the people preserve the sovereign power which formed the basis of the original transfer. I need add no more.

The bases and rights of dominion being thus displayed, we shall readily be able to define private civil right, wrong, justice, and injustice, with their relations to the state; and also to determine what constitutes an ally, or an enemy, or the crime of treason.

By private civil right we can only mean the liberty every man possesses to preserve his existence, a liberty limited by the edicts of the sovereign power, and preserved only by its authority: for when a man has transferred to another his right of living as he likes, which was only limited by his power, that is, has transferred his liberty and power of self-defence, he is bound to live as that other dictates, and to trust him entirely for his defence. Wrong takes place when a citizen, or subject, is forced by another to undergo some loss or pain in contradiction to the authority of the law, or the edict of the sovereign power.

Wrong is conceivable only in an organized community (*in statu civili*) nor can it ever accrue to subjects from any act of the sovereign, from whom all right is derived. It can only arise, therefore, between private persons, who are bound by law and right not to injure one another. Justice consists in the habitual rendering to every man his lawful due: injustice consists in depriving a man, under the pretence of legality, of what the laws, rightly interpreted, would allow him. These last are also called equity and iniquity, because those who administer the laws are bound to show no respect of persons, but to account all men equal, and to defend every man's right equally, neither envying the rich nor despising the poor.

The men of two states become allies, when for the sake of avoiding war, or for some other advantage, they covenant to do each other no hurt, but on the contrary, to assist each other if necessity arises, each retaining his independence. Such a covenant is valid so long as its basis of danger or advantage is in force: no one enters into an engagement, or is bound to stand by his compacts unless there be a hope of some accruing good, or the fear of some evil: if this basis be removed the compact thereby becomes void: this has been abundantly shown by experience. For although different states make treaties not to harm one another, they always take every possible precaution against such treaties being broken by the stronger party, and do not rely on the compact, unless there is a sufficiently obvious object and advantage to both parties in observing it. Otherwise they would fear a breach of faith, nor would there be any wrong done thereby: for who in his proper senses, and aware of the right of the sovereign power, would trust in the promises of one who has the will and the power to do what he likes, and who aims solely at the safety and advantage of his dominion? Moreover, if we consult loyalty and religion, we shall see that no one in possession of power ought to abide by his promises to the injury of his dominion; for he cannot keep such promises without breaking the engagement he made with his subjects, by which both he and they are most solemnly bound.

An enemy is one who lives apart from the state, and does not recognize its authority either as a subject or as an ally. It is not hatred which makes a man an enemy, but the rights of the state. The rights of the state are the same in regard to him who does not recognize by any compact the state authority, as they are against him who has done the state an injury: it has the right to force him as best it can, either to submit, or to contract an alliance.

Lastly, treason can only be committed by subjects, who by compact, either tacit or expressed, have transferred all their rights to the state: a subject is said to have committed this crime when he has attempted, for whatever reason, to seize the sovereign power, or to place it in different hands. I say, *has attempted,* for if punishment were not to overtake him till he had succeeded, it would often come too late, the sovereign rights would have been acquired or transferred already.

I also say, *has attempted, for whatever reason, to seize the sovereign power,* and I recognize no difference whether such an attempt should be followed by public loss or public gain. Whatever be his reason for acting, the crime is treason, and he is rightly condemned: in war, everyone would admit the justice of his sentence. If a man does not keep to his post, but approaches the enemy without the knowledge of his commander, whatever may be his motive, so long as he acts on his own motion, even if he advances with the design of defeating the enemy, he is rightly put to death, because he has violated his oath, and infringed the rights of his commander. That all citizens are equally bound by these rights in time of peace, is not so generally recognized, but the reasons for obedience are, in both cases, identical. The state must be preserved and directed by the sole authority of the sovereign, and such authority and right have been accorded by universal consent to him alone: if, therefore, anyone else attempts, without his consent, to execute any public enterprise, even though the state might (as we said) reap benefit therefrom, such person has none the less infringed the sovereign's right, and would be rightly punished for treason.

In order that every scruple may be removed, we may now

answer the inquiry, whether our former assertion that everyone
who has not the practice of reason, may, in the state of nature,
live by sovereign natural right, according to the laws of his
desires, is not in direct opposition to the law and right of God
as revealed. For as all men absolutely (whether they be less
endowed with reason or more) are equally bound by the
Divine command to love their neighbour as themselves, it may
be said that they cannot, without wrong, do injury to anyone,
or live according to their desires.

This objection, so far as the state of nature is concerned,
can be easily answered, for the state of nature is, both in
nature and in time, prior to religion. No one knows by nature
that he owes any obedience to God,[4] nor can he attain thereto
by any exercise of his reason, but solely by revelation confirmed
by signs. Therefore, previous to revelation, no one is bound by
a Divine law and right of which he is necessarily in ignorance.
The state of nature must by no means be confounded with a
state of religion, but must be conceived as without either religion or law, and consequently without sin or wrong: this is
how we have described it, and we are confirmed by the authority of Paul. It is not only in respect of ignorance that we
conceive the state of nature as prior to, and lacking the Divine
revealed law and right; but in respect of freedom also, wherewith all men are born endowed.

If men were naturally bound by the Divine law and right,
or if the Divine law and right were a natural necessity, there
would have been no need for God to make a covenant with
mankind, and to bind them thereto with an oath and agreement.

We must, then, fully grant that the Divine law and right
originated at the time when men by express covenant agreed
to obey God in all things, and ceded, as it were, their natural

4 See author's note 3, p. 74.

freedom, transferring their rights to God in the manner described in speaking of the formation of a state.

However, I will treat of these matters more at length presently.

It may be insisted that sovereigns (*summæ potestates*) are as much bound by the Divine law as subjects: whereas we have asserted that they retain their natural rights, and may do whatever they like.

In order to clear up the whole difficulty, which arises rather concerning natural right than the state, I maintain that everyone is bound, in the state of nature, to live according to Divine law, in the same way as he is bound to live according to the dictates of sound reason; namely, inasmuch as it is to his advantage, and necessary for his salvation; but, if he will not so live, he may do otherwise at his own risk. He is thus bound to live according to his own laws, not according to anyone else's, and to recognize no man as a judge, or as a superior in religion. Such, in my opinion, is the position of a sovereign, for he may take advice from his fellow-men, but he is not bound to recognize any as a judge, nor anyone besides himself as an arbitrator on any question of right, unless it be a prophet sent expressly by God, and attesting his mission by indisputable signs. Even then he does not recognize a man, but God Himself as His Judge.

If a sovereign (*summa potestas*) refuses to obey God as revealed in His law, he does so at his own risk and loss, but without violating any civil or natural right. For the civil right is dependent on his own decree; and natural right is dependent on the laws of nature, which latter are not adapted to religion, whose sole aim is the good of humanity, but to the order of universal nature—that is, to God's eternal decree unknown to us.

This truth seems to be adumbrated in a somewhat obscurer

form by those who maintain that men can sin against God's revelation, but not against the eternal decree by which He has ordained all things.

We may be asked, what should we do if the sovereign commands anything contrary to religion, and the obedience which we have expressly vowed to God? should we obey the Divine law or the human law? I shall treat of this question at length hereafter, and will therefore merely say now, that God should be obeyed before all else, when we have a certain and indisputable revelation of His will: but men are very prone to error on religious subjects, and, according to the diversity of their dispositions, are wont with considerable stir to put forward their own inventions, as experience more than sufficiently attests, so that if no one were bound to obey the state in matters which, in his own opinion concern religion, the rights of the state would be dependent on every man's judgment and passions. No one would consider himself bound to obey laws framed against his faith or superstition; and on this pretext he might assume unbounded license. In this way, the rights of the civil authorities would be utterly set at nought, so that we must conclude that the sovereign power, which alone is bound both by Divine and natural right to preserve and guard the laws of the state, should have supreme authority for making any laws about religion which it thinks fit; all are bound to obey its behests on the subject in accordance with their promise which God bids them to keep.

However, if the sovereign power be heathen, we should either enter into no engagements therewith, and yield up our lives sooner than transfer to it any of our rights; or, if the engagement be made, and our rights transferred, we should (inasmuch as we should have ourselves transferred the right of defending ourselves and our religion) be bound to obey them, and to keep our word: we might even rightly be bound so to do, except in those cases where God, by indisputable revelation, has promised His special aid against tyranny, or given us special exemption from obedience. Thus we see that, of all the Jews in Babylon, there were only three youths who were certain of the help of God, and, therefore, refused to obey Nebuchadnezzar. All the rest, with the sole exception of Daniel, who was beloved by the king, were doubtless compelled by right to obey, perhaps thinking that they had been delivered up by God into the hands of the king, and that the king had obtained and preserved his dominion by God's design. On the other hand, Eleazar, before his country had utterly fallen, wished to give a proof of his constancy to his compatriots, in order that they might follow in his footsteps, and go to any lengths, rather than allow their right and power to be transferred to the Greeks, or brave any torture rather than swear allegiance to the heathen. Instances are occurring every day in confirmation of what I here advance. The rulers of Christian kingdoms do not hesitate, with a view to strengthening their dominion, to make treaties with Turks and heathen, and to give orders to their subjects who settle among such peoples not to assume more freedom, either in things secular or religious, than is set down in the treaty, or allowed by the foreign government. We may see this exemplified in the Dutch treaty with the Japanese, which I have already mentioned.

Chapter XVII

It Is Shown That No One Can, or Need, Transfer All
His Rights to the Sovereign Power. Of the Hebrew
Republic, as It Was During the Lifetime of Moses,
and after His Death, till the Foundation of the
Monarchy; and of Its Excellence. Lastly, of the Causes
Why the Theocratic Republic Fell, and Why It Could
Hardly Have Continued without Dissension

[In part]

THE theory put forward in the last chapter, of the universal rights of the sovereign power, and of the natural
rights of the individual transferred thereto, though it corresponds in many respects with actual practice, and though practice may be so arranged as to conform to it more and more,
must nevertheless always remain in many respects purely ideal.
No one can ever so utterly transfer to another his power and,
consequently, his rights, as to cease to be a man; nor can there
ever be a power so sovereign that it can carry out every possible
wish. It will always be vain to order a subject to hate what he
believes brings him advantage, or to love what brings him loss,
or not to be offended at insults, or not to wish to be free from
fear, or a hundred other things of the sort, which necessarily
follow from the laws of human nature. So much, I think, is
abundantly shown by experience: for men have never so far
ceded their power as to cease to be an object of fear to the

rulers who received such power and right; and dominions have always been in as much danger from their own subjects as from external enemies. If it were really the case that men could be deprived of their natural rights so utterly as never to have any further influence on affairs, except with the permission of the holders of sovereign right, it would then be possible to maintain with impunity the most violent tyranny, which, I suppose, no one would for an instant admit.

We must, therefore, grant that every man retains some part of his right, in dependence on his own decision, and no one else's.

However, in order correctly to understand the extent of the sovereign's right and power, we must take notice that it does not cover only those actions to which it can compel men by fear, but absolutely every action which it can induce men to perform: for it is the fact of obedience, not the motive for obedience, which makes a man a subject.

Whatever be the cause which leads a man to obey the commands of the sovereign, whether it be fear or hope, or love of his country, or any other emotion—the fact remains that the man takes counsel with himself, and nevertheless acts as his sovereign orders. We must not, therefore, assert that all actions resulting from a man's deliberation with himself are done in obedience to the rights of the individual rather than the sovereign: as a matter of fact, all actions spring from a man's deliberation with himself, whether the determining motive be love or fear of punishment; therefore, either dominion does not exist, and has no rights over its subjects, or else it extends over every instance in which it can prevail on men to decide to obey it. Consequently, every action which a subject performs in accordance with the commands of the sovereign, whether such action springs from love, or fear, or (as is more frequently the case) from hope and fear together, or from reverence compounded of fear and admiration, or, indeed, any motive whatever, is performed in virtue of his submission to the sovereign, and not in virtue of his own authority.

This point is made still more clear by the fact that obedience does not consist so much in the outward act as in the mental state of the person obeying; so that he is most under the dominion of another who with his whole heart determines to obey another's commands; and consequently the firmest dominion belongs to the sovereign who has most influence over the minds of his subjects; if those who are most feared possessed the firmest dominion, the firmest dominion would belong to the subjects of a tyrant, for they are always greatly feared by their ruler. Furthermore, though it is impossible to govern the mind as completely as the tongue, nevertheless minds are, to a certain extent, under the control of the sovereign, for he can in many ways bring about that the greatest part of his subjects should follow his wishes in their beliefs, their loves, and their hates. Though such emotions do not arise at the express command of the sovereign they often result (as experience shows) from the authority of his power, and from his direction; in other words, in virtue of his right; we may, therefore, without doing violence to our understanding, conceive men who follow the instigation of their sovereign in their beliefs, their loves, their hates, their contempt, and all other emotions whatsoever.

Though the powers of government, as thus conceived, are sufficiently ample, they can never become large enough to execute every possible wish of their possessors. This, I think, I have already shown clearly enough. The method of forming a dominion which should prove lasting I do not, as I have said, intend to discuss, but in order to arrive at the object I have in view, I will touch on the teaching of Divine revelation to Moses in this respect, and we will consider the history and the success of the Jews, gathering therefrom what should be the chief concessions made by sovereigns to their subjects with a view to the security and increase of their dominion.

That the preservation of a state chiefly depends on the subjects' fidelity and constancy in carrying out the orders they receive, is most clearly taught both by reason and experience; how subjects ought to be guided so as best to preserve their fidelity and virtue is not so obvious. All, both rulers and ruled, are men, and prone to follow after their lusts. The fickle disposition of the multitude almost reduces those who have experience of it to despair, for it is governed solely by emotions, not by reason: it rushes headlong into every enterprise, and is easily corrupted either by avarice or luxury: everyone thinks himself omniscient and wishes to fashion all things to his liking, judging a thing to be just or unjust, lawful or unlawful, according as he thinks it will bring him profit or loss: vanity leads him to despise his equals, and refuse their guidance: envy of superior fame or fortune (for such gifts are never equally distributed) leads him to desire and rejoice in his neighbour's downfall. I need not go through the whole list, everyone knows already how much crime results from disgust at the present—desire for change, headlong anger, and contempt for poverty—and how men's minds are engrossed and kept in turmoil thereby.

To guard against all these evils, and form a dominion where no room is left for deceit; to frame our institutions so that every man, whatever his disposition, may prefer public right to private advantage, this is the task and this the toil. Necessity is often the mother of invention, but she has never yet succeeded in framing a dominion that was in less danger from its own citizens than from open enemies, or whose rulers did not fear the latter less than the former. Witness the state of Rome, invincible by her enemies, but many times conquered and sorely oppressed by her own citizens, especially in the war between Vespasian and Vitellius. (See Tacitus, Hist. bk. iv. for a description of the pitiable state of the city.)

[F]

Chapter XIX

IT IS SHOWN THE RIGHT OVER MATTERS SPIRITUAL LIES WHOLLY WITH THE SOVEREIGN, AND THAT THE OUTWARD FORMS OF RELIGION SHOULD BE IN ACCORDANCE WITH PUBLIC PEACE, IF WE WOULD OBEY GOD ARIGHT

WHEN I said that the possessors of sovereign power have rights over everything, and that all rights are dependent on their decree, I did not merely mean civil rights, but also spiritual rights;[1] of the latter, no less than the former, they ought to be the interpreters and the champions. I wish to draw special attention to this point, and to discuss it fully in this chapter, because many persons deny that the right of deciding religious questions belongs to the sovereign power, and refuse to acknowledge it as the interpreter of Divine right. They accordingly assume full licence to accuse and arraign it, nay, even to excommunicate it from the Church, as Ambrosius treated the Emperor Theodosius in old time. However, I will show later on in this chapter that they take this means of dividing the government, and paving the way to their own ascendency. I wish, however, first to point out that religion acquires its force as law solely from the decrees of the sovereign. God has no special kingdom among men except in so far as He reigns through temporal rulers. Moreover, the rites of religion and the outward observances of piety should be in accordance with the public peace and well-being, and should

---

[1] Spinoza's terms are *jus sacrum* and *jus civile*.

48

therefore be determined by the sovereign power alone. I speak here only of the outward observances of piety and the external rites of religion, not of piety itself, nor of the inward worship of God, nor the means by which the mind is inwardly led to do homage to God in singleness of heart.

Inward worship of God and piety in itself are within the sphere of everyone's private rights, and cannot be alienated (as I showed at the end of Chapter VII.).[2] What I here mean by the kingdom of God is, I think, sufficiently clear from

[2] The following passage from the end of Chapter VII, "Of the Interpretation of Scripture," is that to which Spinoza here refers: ". . . if everyone were free to interpret the laws of his country as he pleased, no state could stand, but would for that very reason be dissolved at once, and public rights would become private rights.

"With religion the case is widely different. Inasmuch as it consists not so much in outward actions as in simplicity and truth of character, it stands outside the sphere of law and public authority. Simplicity and truth of character are not produced by the constraint of laws, nor by the authority of the state, no one the whole world over can be forced or legislated into a state of blessedness; the means required for such a consummation are faithful and brotherly admonition, sound education, and, above all, free use of the individual judgment.

"Therefore, as the supreme right of free thinking, even on religion, is in every man's power, and as it is inconceivable that such power could be alienated, it is also in every man's power to wield the supreme right and authority of free judgment in this behalf, and to explain and interpret religion for himself. The only reason for vesting the supreme authority in the interpretation of law, and judgment on public affairs in the hands of the magistrates, is that it concerns questions of public right. Similarly the supreme authority in explaining religion, and in passing judgment thereon, is lodged with the individual because it concerns questions of individual right. . . . Thus in this way also, we have shown that our method of interpreting Scripture is the best. For as the highest power of Scriptural interpretation belongs to every man, the rule for such interpretation should be nothing but the natural light of reason which is common to all—not any supernatural light nor any external authority; moreover, such a rule ought not to be so difficult that it can only be applied by very skilful philosophers, but should be adapted to the natural and ordinary faculties and capacity of mankind."

what has been said in Chapter XIV.[3] I there showed that a man best fulfils God's law who worships Him, according to His command, through acts of justice and charity; it follows, therefore, that wherever justice and charity have the force of law and ordinance, there is God's kingdom.

I recognize no difference between the cases where God teaches and commands the practice of justice and charity through our natural faculties, and those where He makes special revelations; nor is the form of the revelation of importance so long as such practice is revealed and becomes a sovereign and supreme law to men. If, therefore, I show that justice and charity can only acquire the force of right and law through the rights of rulers, I shall be able readily to arrive at the conclusion (seeing that the rights of rulers are in the possession of the sovereign), that religion can only acquire the force of right by means of those who have the right to command, and that God only rules among men through the instrumentality of earthly potentates. It follows from what has been said, that the practice of justice and charity only acquires the force of law through the rights of the sovereign authority; for we showed in Chapter XVI. that in the state of nature reason has no more rights than desire, but that men living either by the laws of the former or the laws of the latter, possess rights co-extensive with their powers.

For this reason we could not conceive sin to exist in the state of nature, nor imagine God as a judge punishing man's transgressions; but we supposed all things to happen according to the general laws of universal nature, there being no difference between pious and impious, between him that was pure (as Solomon says) and him that was impure, because there was no possibility either of justice or charity.

[3] See the passages from Chapter XIV appended as a note at the end of Preface, above, pp. 13-16.

In order that the true doctrines of reason, that is (as we showed in Chapter IV.), the true Divine doctrines might obtain absolutely the force of law and right, it was necessary that each individual should cede his natural right, and transfer it either to society as a whole, or to a certain body of men, or to one man. Then, and not till then, does it first dawn upon us what is justice and what is injustice, what is equity and what is iniquity.

Justice, therefore, and absolutely all the precepts of reason, including love towards one's neighbour, receive the force of laws and ordinances solely through the rights of dominion, that is (as we showed in the same chapter) solely on the decree of those who possess the right to rule. Inasmuch as the kingdom of God consists entirely in rights applied to justice and charity or to true religion, it follows that (as we asserted) the kingdom of God can only exist among men through the means of the sovereign powers; nor does it make any difference whether religion be apprehended by our natural faculties or by revelation: the argument is sound in both cases, inasmuch as religion is one and the same, and is equally revealed by God, whatever be the manner in which it becomes known to men.

Thus, in order that the religion revealed by the prophets might have the force of law among the Jews, it was necessary that every man of them should yield up his natural right, and that all should, with one accord, agree that they would only obey such commands as God should reveal to them through the prophets. Just as we have shown to take place in a democracy, where men with one consent agree to live according to the dictates of reason. Although the Hebrews furthermore transferred their right to God, they were able to do so rather in theory than in practice, for, as a matter of fact (as we pointed out above) they absolutely retained the right of dominion till they transferred it to Moses, who in his turn became absolute king, so that it was only through him that God reigned over the Hebrews. For this reason (namely, that religion only acquires the force of law by means of the sovereign power) Moses was not able to punish those who, before the covenant, and consequently while still in possession of their rights, violated the Sabbath (Exod. xvi. 27), but was able to do so after the covenant (Numb. xv. 36), because everyone had then yielded up his natural rights, and the ordinance of the Sabbath had received the force of law.

Lastly, for the same reason, after the destruction of the Hebrew dominion, revealed religion ceased to have the force of law; for we cannot doubt that as soon as the Jews transferred their right to the king of Babylon, the kingdom of God and the Divine right forthwith ceased. For the covenant wherewith they promised to obey all the utterances of God was abrogated; God's kingdom, which was based thereupon, also ceased. The Hebrews could no longer abide thereby, inasmuch as their rights no longer belonged to them but to the king of Babylon, whom (as we showed in Chapter XVI.) they were bound to obey in all things. Jeremiah (chap. xxix. verse 7) expressly admonishes them of this fact: "And seek the peace of the city, whither I have caused you to be carried away captives, and pray unto the Lord for it; for in the peace thereof shall ye have peace." Now, they could not seek the peace of the city as having a share in its government, but only as slaves, being, as they were, captives; by obedience in all things, with a view to avoiding seditions, and by observing all the laws of the country, however different from their own. It is thus abundantly evident that religion among the Hebrews only acquired the form of law through the right of the sovereign rule; when that rule was destroyed, it could no longer be received as the law of a particular kingdom, but only as the universal precept of reason. I say of reason, for the universal religion had not yet become known by revelation. We may therefore draw the general conclusion that religion, whether revealed through our natural faculties or through prophets, receives the force of a command solely through the decrees of the holders of sovereign power; and, further, that God has no special kingdom among men, except in so far as He reigns through earthly potentates.

We may now see in a clearer light what was stated in Chapter IV., namely, that all the decrees of God involve eternal truth and necessity, so that we cannot conceive God as a prince or legislator giving laws to mankind. For this reason the Divine precepts, whether revealed through our natural faculties, or through prophets, do not receive immediately from God the force of a command, but only from those, or through the mediation of those, who possess the right of ruling and legislating. It is only through these latter means that God rules among men, and directs human affairs with justice and equity.

This conclusion is supported by experience, for we find traces of Divine justice only in places where just men bear sway; elsewhere the same lot (to repeat again Solomon's words) befalls the just and the unjust, the pure and the impure: a state of things which causes Divine Providence to be doubted by many who think that God immediately reigns among men, and directs all nature for their benefit.

As, then, both reason and experienec tell us that the Divine right is entirely dependent on the decrees of secular rulers, it follows that secular rulers are its proper interpreters. How this is so we shall now see, for it is time to show that the outward observances of religion, and all the external practices of piety should be brought into accordance with the public peace and well-being if we would obey God rightly. When this has been shown we shall easily understand how the sovereign rulers are the proper interpreters of religion and piety.

It is certain that duties towards one's country are the highest that man can fulfil; for, if government be taken away, no good thing can last, all falls into dispute, anger and anarchy reign unchecked amid universal fear. Consequently there can be no duty towards our neighbour which would not become an offence if it involved injury to the whole state, nor can there be any offence against our duty towards our neighbour, or anything but loyalty in what we do for the sake of preserving the state. For instance: it is in the abstract my duty when my neighbour quarrels with me and wishes to take my cloak, to give him my coat also; but if it be thought that such conduct is hurtful to the maintenance of the state, I ought to bring him to trial, even at the risk of his being condemned to death.

For this reason Manlius Torquatus is held up to honour, inasmuch as the public welfare outweighed with him his duty towards his children. This being so, it follows that the public welfare is the sovereign law to which all others, Divine and human, should be made to conform.

Now, it is the function of the sovereign only to decide what is necessary for the public welfare and the safety of the state, and to give orders accordingly; therefore it is also the function of the sovereign only to decide the limits of our duty towards our neighbour—in other words, to determine how we should obey God. We can now clearly understand how the sovereign is the interpreter of religion, and further, that no one can obey God rightly, if the practices of his piety do not conform to the public welfare; or, consequently, if he does not implicitly obey all the commands of the sovereign. For as by God's command we are bound to do our duty to all men without exception, and to do no man an injury, we are also bound not to help one man at another's loss, still less at a loss to the whole state. Now, no private citizen can know what is good for the state, except he learn it through the sovereign power, who

alone has the right to transact public business: therefore no one
can rightly practise piety or obedience to God, unless he obey
the sovereign power's commands in all things. This proposition
is confirmed by the facts of experience. For if the sovereign
adjudge a man to be worthy of death or an enemy, whether
he be a citizen or a foreigner, a private individual or a separate ruler, no subject is allowed to give him assistance. So
also though the Jews were bidden to love their fellow-citizens as
themselves (Levit. xix. 17, 18), they were nevertheless bound, if
a man offended against the law, to point him out to the judge
(Levit. v. 1, and Deut. xiii. 8, 9), and, if he should be condemned to death, to slay him (Deut. xvii. 7).

Further, in order that the Hebrews might preserve the liberty
they had gained, and might retain absolute sway over the territory they had conquered, it was necessary, as we showed in
Chapter XVII., that their religion should be adapted to their
particular government, and that they should separate themselves from the rest of the nations: wherefore it was commanded to them, "Love thy neighbour and hate thine enemy"
(Matt. v. 43), but after they had lost their dominion and had
gone into captivity in Babylon, Jeremiah bid them take thought
for the safety of the state into which they had been led captive;
and Christ when He saw that they would be spread over the
whole world, told them to do their duty by all men without
exception; all of which instances show that religion has always
been made to conform to the public welfare. Perhaps someone
will ask: By what right, then, did the disciples of Christ, being
private citizens, preach a new religion? I answer that they did
so by the right of the power which they had received from
Christ against unclean spirits (see Matt. x. 1). I have already
stated in Chapter XVI. that all are bound to obey a tryrant,
unless they have received from God through undoubted revelation a promise of aid against him; so let no one take example

from the Apostles unless he too has the power of working miracles. The point is brought out more clearly by Christ's command to His disciples, "Fear not those who kill the body" (Matt. x. 28). If this command were imposed on everyone, governments would be founded in vain, and Solomon's words (Prov. xxiv. 21), "My son, fear God and the king," would be impious, which they certainly are not; we must therefore admit that the authority which Christ gave to His disciples was given to them only, and must not be taken as an example for others.

I do not pause to consider the arguments of those who wish to separate secular rights from spiritual rights, placing the former under the control of the sovereign, and the latter under the control of the universal Church; such pretensions are too frivolous to merit refutation. I cannot, however, pass over in silence the fact that such persons are woefully deceived when they seek to support their seditious opinions (I ask pardon for the somewhat harsh epithet) by the example of the Jewish high priest, who, in ancient times, had the right of administering the sacred offices. Did not the high priests receive their right by the decree of Moses (who, as I have shown, retained the sole right to rule), and could they not by the same means be deprived of it? Moses himself chose not only Aaron, but also his son Eleazar, and his grandson Phineas, and bestowed on them the right of administering the office of high priest. This right was retained by the high priests afterwards, but none the less were they delegates of Moses—that is, of the sovereign power. Moses, as we have shown, left no successor to his dominion, but so distributed his prerogatives, that those who came after him seemed, as it were, regents who administer the government when a king is absent but not dead.

In the second commonwealth the high priests held their right absolutely, after they had obtained the rights of principality in addition. Wherefore the rights of the high priesthood always depended on the edict of the sovereign, and the high priests did not possess them till they became sovereigns also. Rights in matters spiritual always remained under the control of the kings absolutely (as I will show at the end of this chapter), except in the single particular that they were not allowed to administer in person the sacred duties in the Temple, inasmuch as they were not of the family of Aaron, and were therefore considered unclean, a reservation which would have no force in a Christian community.

We cannot, therefore, doubt that the daily sacred rites (whose performance does not require a particular genealogy but only a special mode of life, and from which the holders of sovereign power are not excluded as unclean) are under the sole control of the sovereign power; no one, save by the authority or concession of such sovereign, has the right or power of administering them, of choosing others to administer them, of defining or strengthening the foundations of the Church and her doctrines; of judging on questions of morality or acts of piety; of receiving anyone into the Church or excommunicating him therefrom, or, lastly, of providing for the poor.

These doctrines are proved to be not only true (as we have already pointed out), but also of primary necessity for the preservation of religion and the state. We all know what weight spiritual right and authority carries in the popular mind: how everyone hangs on the lips, as it were, of those who possess it. We may even say that those who wield such authority have the most complete sway over the popular mind.

Whosoever, therefore, wishes to take this right away from the sovereign power, is desirous of dividing the dominion; from such division, contentions, and strife will necessarily spring up, as they did of old between the Jewish kings and high priests, and will defy all attempts to allay them. Nay, further, he who strives to deprive the sovereign power of such authority, is aiming (as we have said), at gaining dominion for himself. What is left for the sovereign power to decide on, if this right be denied him? Certainly nothing concerning either war or peace, if he has to ask another man's opinion as to whether what he believes to be beneficial would be pious or impious. Everything would depend on the verdict of him who had the right of deciding and judging what was pious or impious, right or wrong.

When such a right was bestowed on the Pope of Rome absolutely, he gradually acquired complete control over the kings, till at last he himself mounted to the summits of dominion; however much monarchs, and especially the German emperors, strove to curtail his authority, were it only by a hair's-breadth, they effected nothing, but on the contrary by their very endeavours largely increased it. That which no monarch could accomplish with fire and sword, ecclesiastics could bring about with a stroke of the pen; whereby we may easily see the force and power at the command of the Church, and also how necessary it is for sovereigns to reserve such prerogatives for themselves.

If we reflect on what was said in the last chapter we shall see that such reservation conduced not a little to the increase of religion and piety; for we observed that the prophets themselves, though gifted with Divine efficacy, being merely private citizens, rather irritated than reformed the people by their freedom of warning, reproof, and denunciation, whereas the kings by warnings and punishments easily bent men to their will. Furthermore, the kings themselves, not possessing the right in question absolutely, very often fell away from religion and took with them nearly the whole people. The same thing has often happened from the same cause in Christian states.

Perhaps I shall be asked, "But if the holders of sovereign power choose to be wicked, who will be the rightful champion of piety? Should the sovereigns still be its interpreters?" I meet them with the counter-question, "But if ecclesiastics (who are also human, and private citizens, and who ought to mind only their own affairs), or if others whom it is proposed to entrust with spiritual authority, choose to be wicked, should they still be considered as piety's rightful interpreters?" It is quite certain that when sovereigns wish to follow their own pleasure, whether they have control over spiritual matters or not, the whole state, spiritual and secular, will go to ruin, and it will go much faster if private citizens seditiously assume the championship of the Divine rights.

Thus we see that not only is nothing gained by denying such rights to sovereigns, but on the contrary, great evil ensues. For (as happened with the Jewish kings who did not possess such rights absolutely) rulers are thus driven into wickedness, and the injury and loss to the state become certain and inevitable, instead of uncertain and possible. Whether we look to the abstract truth, or the security of states, or the increase of piety, we are compelled to maintain that the Divine right, or the right of control over spiritual matters, depends absolutely on the decree of the sovereign, who is its legitimate interpreter and champion. Therefore the true ministers of God's word are those who teach piety to the people in obedience to the authority of the sovereign rulers by whose decree it has been brought into conformity with the public welfare.

There remains for me to point out the cause for the frequent disputes on the subject of these spiritual rights in Christian states; whereas the Hebrews, so far as I know, never had any doubts about the matter. It seems monstrous that a question so plain and so vitally important should thus have remained undecided, and that the secular rulers could never obtain the prerogative without controversy, nay, nor without great danger of sedition and injury to religion. If no cause for this state of things were forthcoming, I could easily persuade myself that all I have said in this chapter is mere theorizing, or a kind of speculative reasoning which can never be of any practical use. However, when we reflect on the beginnings of Christianity the cause at once becomes manifest. The Christian religion was not taught at first by kings, but by private persons, who, against the wishes of those in power, whose subjects they were, were for a long time accustomed to hold meetings in secret churches, to institute and perform sacred rites, and on their own authority to settle and decide on their affairs without regard to the state. When, after the lapse of many years, the religion was taken up by the authorities, the ecclesiastics were obliged to teach it to the emperors themselves as they had defined it: wherefore they easily gained recognition as its teachers and interpreters, and the church pastors were looked upon as vicars of God. The ecclesiastics took good care that the Christian kings should not assume their authority, by prohibiting marriage to the chief ministers of religion and to its highest interpreter. They furthermore effected their purpose by multiplying the dogmas of religion to such an extent and so blending them with philosophy that their chief interpreter was bound to be a skilled philosopher and theologian, and to have leisure for a host of idle speculations: conditions which could only be fulfilled by a private individual with much time on his hands.

Among the Hebrews things were very differently arranged: for their Church began at the same time as their dominion, and Moses, their absolute ruler, taught religion to the people, arranged their sacred rites, and chose their spiritual ministers. Thus the royal authority carried very great weight with the people, and the kings kept a firm hold on their spiritual prerogatives.

Although, after the death of Moses, no one held absolute

sway, yet the power of deciding both in matters spiritual and matters temporal was in the hands of the secular chief, as I have already pointed out. Further, in order that it might be taught religion and piety, the people was bound to consult the supreme judge no less than the high priest (Deut. xvii. 9, 11). Lastly, though the kings had not as much power as Moses, nearly the whole arrangement and choice of the sacred ministry depended on their decision. Thus David arranged the whole service of the Temple (see 1 Chron. xxviii. 11, 12, &c.); from all the Levites he chose twenty-four thousand for the sacred psalms; six thousand of these formed the body from which were chosen the judges and prætors, four thousand were porters, and four thousand to play on instruments (see 1 Chron. xxiii. 4, 5). He further divided them into companies (of whom he chose the chiefs), so that each in rotation, at the allotted time, might perform the sacred rites. The priests he also divided into as many companies; I will not go through the whole catalogue, but refer the reader to 2 Chron. viii. 13, where it is stated, "Then Solomon offered burnt offerings to the Lord ... after a certain rate every day, offering according to the commandments of Moses;" and in verse 14, "And he appointed, according to the order of David his father, the courses of the priests to their service ... for so had David the man of God commanded." Lastly, the historian bears witness in verse 15: "And they departed not from the commandment of the king unto the priests and Levites concerning any matter, or concerning the treasuries."

From these and other histories of the kings it is abundantly evident, that the whole practice of religion and the sacred ministry depended entirely on the commands of the king.

When I said above that the kings had not the same right as Moses to elect the high priest, to consult God without inter-mediaries, and to condemn the prophets who prophesied dur-

ing their reign; I said so simply because the prophets
in virtue of their mission, choose a new king and giv
lution for regicide, not because they could call a ki
offended against the law to judgment, or could rigl
against him.[4]

Wherefore if there had been no prophets who, in vir
special revelation, could give absolution for regicide, tl
would have possessed absolute rights over all matt
spiritual and temporal. Consequently the rulers of
times, who have no prophets and would not rightly l
in any case to receive them (for they are not subject
law), have absolute possession of the spiritual pr
although they are not celibates, and they will always
if they will refuse to allow religious dogmas to be un
tiplied or confounded with philosophy.

[4] See author's note 4, p. 75.

CHAPTER XX

THAT IN A FREE STATE EVERY MAN MAY THINK WHAT HE LIKES, AND SAY WHAT HE THINKS

IF men's minds were as easily controlled as their tongues, every king would sit safely on his throne, and government by compulsion would cease; for every subject would shape his life according to the intentions of his rulers, and would esteem a thing true or false, good or evil, just or unjust, in obedience to their dictates. However, we have shown already (Chapter XVII.) that no man's mind can possibly lie wholly at the disposition of another, for no one can willingly transfer his natural right of free reason and judgment, or be compelled so to do. For this reason government which attempts to control minds is accounted tyrannical, and it is considered an abuse of sovereignty and a usurpation of the rights of subjects, to seek to prescribe what shall be accepted as true, or rejected as false, or what opinions should actuate men in their worship of God. All these questions fall within a man's natural right, which he cannot abdicate even with his own consent.

I admit that the judgment can be biassed in many ways, and to an almost incredible degree, so that while exempt from direct external control it may be so dependent on another man's words, that it may fitly be said to be ruled by him; but although this influence is carried to great lengths, it has never gone so far as to invalidate the statement, that every man's understanding is his own, and that brains are as diverse as palates.

Moses, not by fraud, but by Divine virtue, gained such a hold over the popular judgment that he was accounted superhuman, and believed to speak and act through the inspiration of the Deity; nevertheless, even he could not escape murmurs and evil interpretations. How much less then can other monarchs avoid them! Yet such unlimited power, if it exists at all, must belong to a monarch, and least of all to a democracy, where the whole or a great part of the people wield authority collectively. This is a fact which I think everyone can explain for himself.

However unlimited, therefore, the power of a sovereign may be, however implicitly it is trusted as the exponent of law and religion, it can never prevent men from forming judgments according to their intellect, or being influenced by any given emotion. It is true that it has the right to treat as enemies all men whose opinions do not, on all subjects, entirely coincide with its own; but we are not discussing its strict rights, but its proper course of action. I grant that it has the right to rule in the most violent manner, and to put citizens to death for very trivial causes, but no one supposes it can do this with the approval of sound judgment. Nay, inasmuch as such things cannot be done without extreme peril to itself, we may even deny that it has the absolute power to do them, or, consequently, the absolute right; for the rights of the sovereign are limited by his power.

Since, therefore, no one can abdicate his freedom of judgment and feeling; since every man is by indefeasible natural right the master of his own thoughts, it follows that men thinking in diverse and contradictory fashions, cannot, without disastrous results, be compelled to speak only according to the dictates of the supreme power. Not even the most experienced, to say nothing of the multitude, know how to keep silence. Men's common failing is to confide their plans to others, though there be need for secrecy, so that a government would be most harsh which deprived the individual of his freedom of saying and teaching what he thought; and would be moderate if such freedom were granted. Still we cannot deny that authority may be as much injured by words as by actions; hence, although the freedom we are discussing cannot be entirely denied to subjects, its unlimited concession would be most baneful; we must, therefore, now inquire, how far such freedom can and ought to be conceded without danger to the peace of the state, or the power of the rulers; and this, as I said at the beginning of Chapter XVI., is my principal object.

It follows, plainly, from the explanation given above, of the foundations of a state, that the ultimate aim of government is not to rule, or restrain, by fear, nor to exact obedience, but contrariwise, to free every man from fear, that he may live in all possible security; in other words, to strengthen his natural right to exist and work without injury to himself or others.

No, the object of government is not to change men from rational beings into beasts or puppets, but to enable them to develop their minds and bodies in security, and to employ their reason unshackled; neither showing hatred, anger, or deceit, nor watched with the eyes of jealousy and injustice. In fact, the true aim of government is liberty.

Now we have seen that in forming a state the power of making laws must either be vested in the body of the citizens, or in a portion of them, or in one man. For, although men's free judgments are very diverse, each one thinking that he alone knows everything, and although complete unanimity of feeling and speech is out of the question, it is impossible to preserve peace, unless individuals abdicate their right of acting entirely on their own judgment. Therefore, the individual justly cedes the right of free action, though not of free reason and judgment; no one can act against the authorities without danger to the state, though his feelings and judgment may be at variance therewith; he may even speak against them, provided that he does so from rational conviction, not from fraud, anger, or hatred, and provided that he does not attempt to introduce any change on his private authority.

For instance, supposing a man shows that a law is repugnant to sound reason, and should therefore be repealed; if he submits his opinion to the judgment of the authorities (who, alone, have the right of making and repealing laws), and meanwhile acts in nowise contrary to that law, he has deserved well of the state, and has behaved as a good citizen should; but if he accuses the authorities of injustice, and stirs up the people against them, or if he seditiously strives to abrogate the law without their consent, he is a mere agitator and rebel.

Thus we see how an individual may declare and teach what he believes, without injury to the authority of his rulers, or to the public peace; namely, by leaving in their hands the entire power of legislation as it affects action, and by doing nothing against their laws, though he be compelled often to act in contradiction to what he believes, and openly feels, to be best.

Such a course can be taken without detriment to justice and dutifulness, nay, it is the one which a just and dutiful man would adopt. We have shown that justice is dependent on the laws of the authorities, so that no one who contravenes their accepted decrees can be just, while the highest regard for duty, as we have pointed out in the preceding chapter, is exercised in maintaining public peace and tranquillity; these could not be preserved if every man were to live as he pleased; therefore it is no less than undutiful for a man to act contrary to his country's laws, for if the practice became universal the ruin of states would necessarily follow.

Hence, so long as a man acts in obedience to the laws of his rulers, he in nowise contravenes his reason, for in obedience to reason he transferred the right of controlling his actions from his own hands to theirs. This doctrine we can confirm from actual custom, for in a conference of great and small powers, schemes are seldom carried unanimously, yet all unite in carrying out what is decided on, whether they voted for or against. But I return to my proposition.

From the fundamental notions of a state, we have discovered how a man may exercise free judgment without detriment to the supreme power: from the same premises we can no less easily determine what opinions would be seditious. Evidently those which by their very nature nullify the compact by which the right of free action was ceded. For instance, a man who holds that the supreme power has no rights over him, or that promises ought not to be kept, or that everyone should live as he pleases, or other doctrines of this nature in direct opposition to the above-mentioned contract, is seditious, not so much from his actual opinions and judgment, as from the deeds which they involve; for he who maintains such theories abrogates the contract which tacitly, or openly, he made with his rulers. Other opinions which do not involve acts violating the contract, such as revenge, anger, and the like, are not seditious, unless it be in some corrupt state, where superstitious and ambitious persons, unable to endure men of learning, are so popular with the multitude that their word is more valued than the law.

However, I do not deny that there are some doctrines which, while they are apparently only concerned with abstract truths and falsehoods, are yet propounded and published with unworthy motives. This question we have discussed in Chapter XV., and shown that reason should nevertheless remain unshackled. If we hold to the principle that a man's loyalty to the state should be judged, like his loyalty to God, from his actions only—namely, from his charity towards his neighbours; we cannot doubt that the best government will allow freedom of philosophical speculation no less than of religious belief. I confess that from such freedom inconveniences may sometimes arise, but what question was ever settled so wisely that no abuses could possibly spring therefrom? He who seeks to regulate everything by law, is more likely to arouse vices than to reform them. It is best to grant what cannot be abolished, even though it be in itself harmful. How many evils spring from luxury, envy, avarice, drunkenness, and the like, yet these are tolerated—vices as they are—because they cannot be prevented by legal enactments. How much more then should free thought be granted, seeing that it is in itself a virtue and that it cannot be crushed! Besides, the evil results can easily be checked, as I will show, by the secular authorities, not to mention that such freedom is absolutely necessary for progress in science and the liberal arts: for no man follows such pursuits to advantage unless his judgment be entirely free and unhampered.

But let it be granted that freedom may be crushed, and men be so bound down, that they do not dare to utter a whisper, save at the bidding of their rulers; nevertheless this can never be carried to the pitch of making them think according to authority, so that the necessary consequences would be that men would daily be thinking one thing and saying another, to the corruption of good faith, that mainstay of government, and to the fostering of hateful flattery and perfidy, whence spring stratagems, and the corruption of every good art.

It is far from possible to impose uniformity of speech, for the more rulers strive to curtail freedom of speech, the more obstinately are they resisted; not indeed by the avaricious, the flatterers, and other numskulls, who think supreme salvation consists in filling their stomachs and gloating over their money-bags, but by those whom good education, sound morality, and virtue have rendered more free. Men, as generally constituted, are most prone to resent the branding as criminal of opinions which they believe to be true, and the proscription as wicked of that which inspires them with piety towards God and man; hence they are ready to forswear the laws and conspire against the authorities, thinking it not shameful but honourable to stir up seditions and perpetuate any sort of crime with this end in view. Such being the constitution of human nature, we see that laws directed against opinions affect the generous-minded rather than the wicked, and are adapted less for coercing criminals than for irritating the upright; so that they cannot be maintained without great peril to the state.

Moreover, such laws are almost always useless, for those who hold that the opinions proscribed are sound, cannot possibly obey the law; whereas those who already reject them as false, accept the law as a kind of privilege, and make such boast of it, that authority is powerless to repeal it, even if such a course be subsequently desired.

To these considerations may be added what we said in Chapter XVIII. in treating of the history of the Hebrews. And, lastly, how many schisms have arisen in the Church from the attempt of the authorities to decide by law the intricacies of theological controversy! If men were not allured by the hope of getting the law and the authorities on their side, of triumphing over their adversaries in the sight of an applauding multitude, and of acquiring honourable distinctions, they would not strive so maliciously, nor would such fury sway their minds. This is taught not only by reason but by daily examples, for laws of this kind prescribing what every man shall believe and forbidding anyone to speak or write to the contrary, have often been passed, as sops or concessions to the anger of those who cannot tolerate men of enlightenment, and who, by such harsh and crooked enactments, can easily turn the devotion of the masses into fury and direct it against whom they will.

How much better would it be to restrain popular anger and

fury, instead of passing useless laws, which can only be broken by those who love virtue and the liberal arts, thus paring down the state till it is too small to harbour men of talent. What greater misfortune for a state can be conceived than that honourable men should be sent like criminals into exile, because they hold diverse opinions which they cannot disguise? What, I say, can be more hurtful than that men who have committed no crime or wickedness should, simply because they are enlightened, be treated as enemies and put to death, and that the scaffold, the terror of evil-doers, should become the arena where the highest examples of tolerance and virtue are displayed to the people with all the marks of ignominy that authority can devise?

He that knows himself to be upright does not fear the death of a criminal, and shrinks from no punishment; his mind is not wrung with remorse for any disgraceful deed: he holds that death in a good cause is no punishment, but an honour, and that death for freedom is glory.

What purpose then is served by the death of such men, what example is proclaimed? the cause for which they die is unknown to the idle and the foolish, hateful to the turbulent, loved by the upright. The only lesson we can draw from such scenes is to flatter the persecutor, or else to imitate the victim.

If formal assent is not to be esteemed above conviction, and if governments are to retain a firm hold of authority and not be compelled to yield to agitators, it is imperative that freedom of judgment should be granted, so that men may live together in harmony, however diverse, or even openly contradictory their opinions may be. We cannot doubt that such is the best system of government and open to the fewest objections, since it is the one most in harmony with human nature. In a democracy (which most closely approaches the natural state) everyone submits to the control of authority over his actions, but not over his judgment and reason; that is, seeing that all cannot think alike, the voice of the majority has the force of law, subject to repeal if circumstances bring about a change of opinion. In proportion as the power of free judgment is withheld we depart from the natural condition of mankind, and consequently the government becomes more tyrannical.

In order to prove that from such freedom no inconvenience arises, which cannot easily be checked by the exercise of the sovereign power, and that men's actions can easily be kept in bounds, though their opinions be at open variance, it will be well to cite an example. Such an one is not very far to seek. The city of Amsterdam reaps the fruit of this freedom in its own great prosperity and in the admiration of all other people. For in this most flourishing state, and most splendid city, men of every nation and religion live together in the greatest harmony, and ask no questions before trusting their goods to a fellow-citizen, save whether he be rich or poor, and whether he generally acts honestly, or the reverse. His religion and sect is considered of no importance: for it has no effect before the judges in gaining or losing a cause, and there is no sect so despised that its followers, provided that they harm no one, pay every man his due, and live uprightly, are deprived of the protection of the magisterial authority.

On the other hand, when the religious controversy between Remonstrants and Counter-Remonstrants began to be taken up by politicians and the States, it grew into a schism, and abundantly showed that laws dealing with religion and seeking to settle its controversies are much more calculated to irritate than to reform, and that they give rise to extreme licence: further, it was seen that schisms do not originate in a love of truth, which is a source of courtesy and gentleness, but rather in an inordinate desire for supremacy. From all these considerations it is clearer than the sun at noonday, that the true schismatics

are those who condemn other men's writings, and seditiously
stir up the quarrelsome masses against their authors, rather
than those authors themselves, who generally write only for the
learned, and appeal solely to reason. In fact, the real disturbers
of the peace are those who, in a free state, seek to curtail the
liberty of judgment which they are unable to tyrannize over.

I have thus shown:—I. That it is impossible to deprive men
of the liberty of saying what they think. II. That such liberty
can be conceded to every man without injury to the rights and
authority of the sovereign power, and that every man may
retain it without injury to such rights, provided that he does
not presume upon it to the extent of introducing any new
rights into the state, or acting in any way contrary to the
existing laws. III. That every man may enjoy this liberty without detriment to the public peace, and that no inconveniences
arise therefrom which cannot easily be checked. IV. That every
man may enjoy it without injury to his allegiance. V. That
laws dealing with speculative problems are entirely useless.
VI. Lastly, that not only may such liberty be granted without
prejudice to the public peace, to loyalty, and to the rights of
rulers, but that it is even necessary for their preservation. For
when people try to take it away, and bring to trial, not only
the acts which alone are capable of offending, but also the
opinions of mankind, they only succeed in surrounding their
victims with an appearance of martyrdom, and raise feelings
of pity and revenge rather than of terror. Uprightness and good
faith are thus corrupted, flatterers and traitors are encouraged,
and sectarians triumph, inasmuch as concessions have been
made to their animosity, and they have gained the state sanction for the doctrines of which they are the interpreters. Hence
they arrogate to themselves the state authority and rights, and
do not scruple to assert that they have been directly chosen by
God, and that their laws are Divine, whereas the laws of the

state are human, and should therefore yield obedience to the laws of God—in other words, to their own laws. Everyone must see that this is not a state of affairs conducive to public welfare. Wherefore, as we have shown in Chapter XVIII., the safest way for a state is to lay down the rule that religion is comprised solely in the exercise of charity and justice, and that the rights of rulers in sacred, no less than in secular matters, should merely have to do with actions, but that every man should think what he likes and say what he thinks.

I have thus fulfilled the task I set myself in this treatise. It remains only to call attention to the fact that I have written nothing which I do not most willingly submit to the examination and approval of my country's rulers; and that I am willing to retract anything which they shall decide to be repugnant to the laws, or prejudicial to the public good. I know that I am a man, and as a man liable to error, but against error I have taken scrupulous care, and have striven to keep in entire accordance with the laws of my country, with loyalty, and with morality.

AUTHOR'S NOTES

CHAPTER XVI

1. In the state of social life, where general right determines what is good or evil, stratagem is rightly distinguished as of two kinds, good and evil. But in the state of Nature, where every man is his own judge, possessing the absolute right to lay down laws for himself, to interpret them as he pleases, or to abrogate them if he thinks it convenient, it is not conceivable that stratagem should be evil.

2. Whatever be the social state a man finds himself in, he may be free. For certainly a man is free, in so far as he is led by reason. Now reason (though Hobbes thinks otherwise) is always on the side of peace, which cannot be attained unless the general laws of the state be respected. Therefore the more a man is led by reason—in other words, the more he is free, the more constantly will he respect the laws of his country, and obey the commands of the sovereign power to which he is subject.

3. When Paul says that men have in themselves no refuge, he speaks as a man: for in the ninth chapter of the same epistle he expressly teaches that God has mercy on whom He will, and that men are without excuse, only because they are in God's power like clay in the hands of a potter, who out of the same lump makes vessels, some for honour and some for dishonour, not because they have been forewarned. As regards the Divine natural law whereof the chief commandment is, as we have said, to love God, I have called it a law in the same sense, as philosophers style laws those general rules of nature, according to which everything happens. For the love of God is not a state of obedience: it is a virtue which necessarily exists in a man who knows God rightly. Obedience has regard to the will of a

ruler, not to necessity and truth. Now as we are ignorant of the nature of God's will, and on the other hand know that everything happens solely by God's power, we cannot, except through revelation, know whether God wishes in any way to be honoured as a sovereign.

Again; we have shown that the Divine rights appear to us in the light of rights or commands, only so long as we are ignorant of their cause: as soon as their cause is known, they cease to be rights, and we embrace them no longer as rights but as eternal truths; in other words, obedience passes into love of God, which emanates from true knowledge as necessarily as light emanates from the sun. Reason then leads us to love God, but cannot lead us to obey Him; for we cannot embrace the commands of God as Divine, while we are in ignorance of their cause, neither can we rationally conceive God as a sovereign laying down laws as a sovereign.

CHAPTER XIX

4. I must here bespeak special attention for what was said in Chap. XVI. concerning rights.

BENEDICT DE SPINOZA'S POLITICAL TREATISE

WHEREIN IS DEMONSTRATED, HOW THE SOCIETY IN
WHICH MONARCHICAL DOMINION FINDS PLACE,
AS ALSO THAT IN WHICH THE DOMINION
IS ARISTOCRATIC, SHOULD BE ORDERED,
SO AS NOT TO LAPSE INTO A
TYRANNY, BUT TO PRESERVE
INVIOLATE THE PEACE
AND FREEDOM OF
THE CITIZENS

(TRACTATUS POLITICUS)

[A]

"Letter of the Author to a Friend, Which May Properly Be Prefixed to This Political Treatise, and Serve It for a Preface"

"DEAR Friend,—Your welcome letter was delivered to me yesterday. I heartily thank you for the kind interest you take in me. I would not miss this opportunity, were I not engaged in something, which I think more useful, and which, I believe, will please you more—that is, in preparing a Political Treatise, which I began some time since, upon your advice. Of this treatise, six chapters are already finished. The first contains a kind of introduction to the actual work; the second treats of natural right; the third, of the right of supreme authorities. In the fourth, I inquire, what political matters are subject to the direction of supreme authorities; in the fifth, what is the ultimate and highest end which a society can contemplate; and, in the sixth, how a monarchy should be ordered, so as not to lapse into a tyranny. I am at present writing the seventh chapter, wherein I make a regular demonstration of all the heads of my preceding sixth chapter, concerning the ordering of a well-regulated monarchy. I shall afterwards pass to the subjects of aristocratic and popular dominion, and, lastly, to that of laws and other particular questions about politics. And so, farewell."

[B]

A Political Treatise
(Tractatus Politicus)

Chapter I

Introduction

PHILOSOPHERS conceive of the passions which harass us as vices into which men fall by their own fault, and, therefore, generally deride, bewail, or blame them, or execrate them, if they wish to seem unusually pious. And so they think they are doing something wonderful, and reaching the pinnacle of learning, when they are clever enough to bestow manifold praise on such human nature, as is nowhere to be found, and to make verbal attacks on that which, in fact, exists. For they conceive of men, not as they are, but as they themselves would like them to be. Whence it has come to pass that, instead of ethics, they have generally written satire, and that they have never conceived a theory of politics, which could be turned to use, but such as might be taken for a chimera, or might have been formed in Utopia, or in that golden age of the poets when, to be sure, there was least need of it. Accordingly, as in all sciences, which have a useful application, so especially in that of politics, theory is supposed to be at variance with practice; and no men are esteemed less fit to direct public affairs than theorists or philosophers.

2. But statesmen, on the other hand, are suspected of plotting against mankind, rather than consulting their interests, and are

esteemed more crafty than learned. No doubt nature has taught them, that vices will exist, while men do. And so, while they study to anticipate human wickedness, and that by arts, which experience and long practice have taught, and which men generally use under the guidance more of fear than of reason, they are thought to be enemies of religion, especially by divines, who believe that supreme authorities should handle public affairs in accordance with the same rules of piety, as bind a private individual. Yet there can be no doubt, that statesmen have written about politics far more happily than philosophers. For, as they had experience for their mistress, they taught nothing that was inconsistent with practice.

3. And, certainly, I am fully persuaded that experience has revealed all conceivable sorts of commonwealth (*civitas*), which are consistent with men's living in unity, and likewise the means by which the multitude may be guided or kept within fixed bounds. So that I do not believe that we can by meditation discover in this matter anything not yet tried and ascertained, which shall be consistent with experience or practice. For men are so situated, that they cannot live without some general law. But general laws and public affairs are ordained and managed by men of the utmost acuteness, or, if you like, of great cunning or craft. And so it is hardly credible, that we should be able to conceive of anything serviceable to a general society (*Societas communis*), that occasion or chance has not offered, or that men, intent upon their common affairs, and seeking their own safety, have not seen for themselves.

4. Therefore, on applying my mind to politics, I have resolved to demonstrate by a certain and undoubted course of argument, or to deduce from the very condition of human nature, not what is new and unheard of, but only such things as agree best with practice. And that I might investigate the subject-matter of this science with the same freedom of spirit

as we generally use in mathematics, I have laboured carefully, not to mock, lament, or execrate, but to understand human actions; and to this end I have looked upon passions, such as love, hatred, anger, envy, ambition, pity, and the other perturbations of the mind, not in the light of vices of human nature, but as properties, just as pertinent to it, as are heat, cold, storm, thunder, and the like to the nature of the atmosphere, which phenomena, though inconvenient, are yet necessary, and have fixed causes, by means of which we endeavour to understand their nature, and the mind has just as much pleasure in viewing them aright, as in knowing such things as flatter the senses.[1]

[1] With this, and the opening paragraph above, compare the following passage from the famous introductory paragraph of the Ethics, Book III.

"Most writers on the emotions and on human conduct seem to be treating rather of matters outside nature than of natural phenomena following nature's general laws. They appear to conceive man to be situated in nature as a kingdom within a kingdom: for they believe that he disturbs rather than follows nature's order, that he has absolute control over his actions, and that he is determined solely by himself. They attribute human infirmities and fickleness, not to the power of nature in general, but to some mysterious flaw in the nature of man, which accordingly they bemoan, deride, despise, or, as usually happens, abuse: he, who succeeds in hitting off the weakness of the human mind more eloquently or more acutely than his fellows, is looked upon as a seer. Still there has been no lack of very excellent men (to whose toil and industry I confess myself much indebted), who have written many noteworthy things concerning the right way of life, and have given much sage advice to mankind. But no one, so far as I know, has defined the nature and strength of the emotions, and the power of the mind against them for their restraint.

"I do not forget, that the illustrious Descartes, though he believed, that the mind has absolute power over its actions, strove to explain human emotions by their primary causes, and, at the same time, to point out a way, by which the mind might attain to absolute dominion over them. However, in my opinion, he accomplishes nothing beyond a display of the acuteness of his own great intellect, as I will show in the proper place. For the present I wish to revert to those, who would rather abuse or deride human emotions than understand them. Such persons will, doubtless, think it strange that I should attempt to treat of human vice and

5. For this is certain, and we have proved its truth in our Ethics,[2] that men are of necessity liable to passions, and so constituted as to pity those who are ill, and envy those who are well off; and to be prone to vengeance more than to mercy: and moreover, that every individual wishes the rest to live after his own mind, and to approve what he approves, and reject what he rejects. And so it comes to pass, that, as all are equally eager to be first, they fall to strife, and do their utmost mutually to oppress one another; and he who comes out conqueror is more proud of the harm he has done to the other, than of the good he has done to himself. And although all are persuaded, that religion, on the contrary, teaches every man to love his neighbour as himself, that is to defend another's right just as much as his own, yet we showed that this persuasion has too little power over the passions. It avails, indeed, in the hour of death, when disease has subdued the very passions,

---

folly geometrically, and should wish to set forth with rigid reasoning those matters which they cry out against as repugnant to reason, frivolous, absurd, and dreadful. However, such is my plan. Nothing comes to pass in nature, which can be set down to a flaw therein; for nature is always the same, and everywhere one and the same in her efficacy and power of action; that is, nature's laws and ordinances, whereby all things come to pass and change from one form to another, are everywhere and always the same; so that there should be one and the same method of understanding the nature of all things whatsoever, namely, through nature's universal laws and rules. Thus the passions of hatred, anger, envy, and so on, considered in themselves, follow from this same necessity and efficacy of nature; they answer to certain definite causes, through which they are understood, and possess certain properties as worthy of being known as the properties of anything else, whereof the contemplation in itself affords us delight. I shall, therefore, treat of the nature and strength of the emotions according to the same method, as I employed heretofore in my investigations concerning God and the mind. I shall consider human actions and desires in exactly the same manner, as though I were concerned with lines, planes, and solids."

[2] Ethics, III, 1; IV, 4. Coroll.; III. 31, note; 32, note; IV. App. 4, 13; IV. 58, note, 15.

and man lies inert, or in temples, where men hold no traffic, but least of all, where it is most needed, in the law-court or the palace. We showed too, that reason can, indeed, do much to restrain and moderate the passions, but we saw at the same time, that the road, which reason herself points out, is very steep; so that such as persuade themselves, that the multitude or men distracted by politics can ever be induced to live according to the bare dictate of reason, must be dreaming of the poetic golden age, or of a stage-play.

6. A dominion (*Imperium*)[3] then, whose well-being depends on any man's good faith, and whose affairs cannot be properly administered, unless those who are engaged in them will act honestly, will be very unstable. On the contrary, to insure its permanence, its public affairs should be so ordered, that those who administer them, whether guided by reason or passion, cannot be led to act treacherously or basely. Nor does it matter to the security of a dominion, in what spirit men are led to rightly administer its affairs. For liberality of spirit, or courage, is a private virtue; but the virtue of a state is its security.

7. Lastly, inasmuch as all men, whether barbarous or civilized, everywhere frame customs, and form some kind of civil state, we must not, therefore, look to proofs of reason for the causes and natural bases of dominion, but derive them from the general nature or condition of mankind, as I mean to do in the next chapter.

[3] Elwes's translation of *imperium,* "dominion" has been retained. Spinoza means by the term the fact of social organization with its principle of authority. "The state" or "government" would be a suitable translation in some cases, but not in all.

CHAPTER II

OF NATURAL RIGHT

IN our Theologico-Politico Treatise we have treated of natural and civil right,[1] and in our Ethics have explained the nature of wrong-doing, merit, justice, injustice,[2] and lastly, of human liberty.[3] Yet, lest the readers of the present treatise should have to seek elsewhere those points, which especially concern it, I have determined to explain them here again, and give a deductive proof of them.

2. Any natural thing whatever can be just as well conceived, whether it exists or does not exist. As then the beginning of the existence of natural things cannot be inferred from their definition, so neither can their continuing to exist. For their ideal essence is the same, after they have begun to exist, as it was before they existed. As then their beginning to exist cannot be inferred from their essence, so neither can their continuing to exist; but they need the same power to enable them to go on existing, as to enable them to begin to exist. From which it follows, that the power, by which natural things exist, and therefore that by which they operate, can be no other than the eternal power of God itself. For were it another and a created power, it could not preserve itself, much less natural things, but it would itself, in order to continue to exist, have need of the same power which it needed to be created.

3. From this fact therefore, that is, that the power whereby

[1] Cf. the selection from Ch. XVI of the T. T.-P., above, pp. 27-42.
[2] Ethics, IV, 37, note 2.
[3] Ethics, IV, 67; II, 48, 49 note.

85

natural things exist and operate is the very power of God itself, we easily understand what natural right (*jus naturae*) is. For as God has a right to everything, and God's right is nothing else, but his very power, as far as the latter is considered to be absolutely free; it follows from this, that every natural thing has by nature as much right, as it has power to exist and operate; since the natural power of every natural thing, whereby it exists and operates, is nothing else but the power of God, which is absolutely free.

4. And so by natural right I understand the very laws or rules of nature, in accordance with which everything takes place, in other words, the power of nature itself. And so the natural right of universal nature, and consequently of every individual thing, extends as far as its power: and accordingly, whatever any man does after the laws of his nature, he does by the highest natural right, and he has as much right according to nature as he has power.[4]

5. If then human nature had been so constituted, that men should live according to the mere dictate of reason, and attempt nothing inconsistent therewith, in that case natural right, considered as special to mankind, would be determined by the power of reason only. But men are more led by blind desire, than by reason: and therefore the natural power or right of human beings should be limited, not by reason, but by every appetite, whereby they are determined to action, or seek their own preservation. I, for my part, admit, that those desires, which arise not from reason, are not so much actions as passive affections (*passiones*) of man. But as we are treating here of the universal power or right of nature, we cannot here recognize any distinction between desires, which are engendered in us by reason, and those which are engendered by other causes; since the latter, as much as the former, are effects of nature,

[4] *Cf.* the selection from Ch. IV of the *T. T.-P.*, above, pp. 17-23.

and display the natural impulse, by which man strives to continue in existence. For man, be he learned or ignorant, is part of nature, and everything, by which any man is determined to action, ought to be referred to the power of nature, that is, to that power, as it is limited by the nature of this or that man. For man, whether guided by reason or desire alone, does nothing save in accordance with the laws and rules of nature, that is, by natural right. (Section 4.)

6. But most people believe, that the ignorant rather disturb than follow the course of nature, and conceive of mankind in nature as of one dominion within another. For they maintain, that the human mind is produced by no natural causes, but created directly by God, and is so independent of other things, that it has an absolute power to determine itself, and make a right use of reason. Experience, however, teaches us but too well, that it is no more in our power to have a sound mind, than a sound body. Next, inasmuch as everything whatever, as far as in it lies, strives to preserve its own existence, we cannot at all doubt, that, were it as much in our power to live after the dictate of reason, as to be led by blind desire, all would be led by reason, and order their lives wisely; which is very far from being the case, for everyone is led by his own pleasure. Nor do divines remove this difficulty, at least not by deciding, that the cause of this want of power is a vice or sin in human nature, deriving its origin from our first parents' fall. For if it was even in the first man's power as much to stand as to fall, and he was in possession of his senses, and had his nature unimpaired, how could it be, that he fell in spite of his knowledge and foresight? But they say, that he was deceived by the devil. Who then was it, that deceived the devil himeslf? Who, I say, so maddened the very being that excelled all other created intelligences, that he wished to be greater than God? For was not *his* effort too, supposing him of sound mind, to

preserve himself and his existence, as far as in him lay? Besides, how could it happen, that the first man himself, being in his senses, and master of his own will, should be led astray, and suffer himself to be taken mentally captive? For if he had the power to make a right use of reason, it was not possible for him to be deceived, for as far as in him lay, he of necessity strove to preserve his existence and his soundness of mind. But the hypothesis is, that he had this in his power; therefore he of necessity maintained his soundness of mind, and could not be deceived. But this from his history, is known to be false. And, accordingly, it must be admitted, that it was not in the first man's power to make a right use of reason, but that, like us, he was subject to passions.

7. But that man, like other beings, as far as in him lies, strives to preserve his existence, no one can deny. For if any distinction could be conceived on this point, it must arise from man's having a free will. But the freer we conceived man to be, the more we should be forced to maintain, that he must of necessity preserve his existence and be in possession of his senses; as anyone will easily grant me, that does not confound liberty with contingency. For liberty is a virtue, or excellence. Whatever, therefore, convicts a man of weakness cannot be ascribed to his liberty. And so man can by no means be called free, because he is able not to exist or not to use his reason, but only in so far as he preserves the power of existing and operating according to the laws of human nature. The more, therefore, we consider man to be free, the less we can say, that he can neglect to use reason, or choose evil in preference to good; and, therefore, God, who exists in absolute liberty, also understands and operates of necessity, that is, exists, understands, and operates according to the necessity of his own nature. For there is no doubt, that God operates by the same liberty whereby he exists. As then he exists by the necessity

of his own nature, by the necessity of his own nature also he acts, that is, he acts with absolute liberty.

8. So we conclude, that it is not in the power of any man always to use his reason, and be at the highest pitch of human liberty, and yet that everyone always, as far as in him lies, strives to preserve his own existence; and that (since each has as much right as he has power) whatever anyone, be he learned or ignorant, attempts and does, he attempts and does by supreme natural right. From which it follows that the law and ordinance of nature, under which all men are born, and for the most part live, forbids nothing but what no one wishes or is able to do, and is not opposed to strifes, hatred, anger, treachery, or, in general, anything that appetite suggests. No wonder in this, for nature is not bound by the laws of human reason, which do but pursue the true interest and preservation of mankind, but by other infinite laws, which regard the eternal order of universal nature, whereof man is an atom; and according to the necessity of this order only are all individual beings determined in a fixed manner to exist and operate. Whenever, then, anything in nature seems to us ridiculous, absurd, or evil, it is because we have but a partial knowledge of things, and are in the main ignorant of the order and coherence of nature as a whole, and because we want everything to be arranged according to the dictate of our own reason; although, in fact, what our reason pronounces bad, is not bad as regards the order and laws of universal nature, but only as regards the laws of our own nature taken separately.

9. Besides, it follows that everyone is so far rightfully dependent on another, as he is under that other's power, and so far independent, as he is able to repel all violence, and avenge to his heart's content all damage done to him, and in general to live after his own mind.

10. He has another under his power, who holds him bound, or has taken from him arms and means of defence or escape, or inspired him with fear, or so attached him to himself by past favour, that the man obliged would rather please his benefactor than himself, and live after his mind than after his own. He that has another under his power in the first or second of these ways, holds but his body, not his mind. But in the third or fourth way he has made dependent on himself as well the mind as the body of the other; yet only as long as the fear or hope lasts, for upon the removal of the feeling the other is left independent.

11. The faculty of judgment can be dependent on another, only as far as that other can deceive the mind; whence it follows that the mind is so far independent, as it uses reason aright. Nay, inasmuch as human power is to be reckoned less by physical vigour than by mental strength, it follows that those men are most independent whose reason is strongest, and who are most guided thereby. And so I am altogether for calling a man so far free, as he is led by reason; because so far he is determined to action by such causes, as can be adequately understood by his own nature, although by these causes he be necessarily determined to action. For liberty, as we showed above (Sec. 7), does not take away the necessity of acting, but supposes it.

12. The pledging of faith to any man, where one has but verbally promised to do this or that, which one might rightfully leave undone, or *vice versâ,* remains so long valid as the will of him that gave his word remains unchanged. For he that has power to break faith has, in fact, bated nothing of his own right, but only made a present of words. If, then, he, being by natural right judge in his own case, comes to the conclusion, rightly or wrongly (for "to err is human"), that more harm than profit will come of his promise, by the judgment of his

own mind he decides that the promise should be broken, and by natural right (Sec. 9) he will break the same.

13. If two come together and unite their strength, they have jointly more power, and consequently more right according to nature than both of them separately, and the more there are that have so joined in alliance, the more right they all collectively will possess.

14. In so far as men are tormented by anger, envy, or any passion implying hatred, they are drawn asunder and made contrary one to another, and therefore are so much the more to be feared, as they are more powerful, crafty, and cunning than the other animals. And because men are in the highest degree liable to these passions (Chap. I, Sec. 5), therefore men are naturally enemies. For he is my greatest enemy, whom I must most fear and be on my guard against.

15. But inasmuch as (Sec. 6) in the state of nature each is so long independent, as he can guard against oppression by another, and it is in vain for one man alone to try and guard against all, it follows hence that so long as the natural right of man is determined by the power of every individual, and belongs to everyone, so long it is a nonentity, existing in opinion rather than fact, as there is no assurance of making it good. And it is certain that the greater cause of fear every individual has, the less power, and consequently the less right, he possesses. To this must be added, that without mutual help men can hardly support life and cultivate the mind. And so our conclusion is, that that natural right, which is special to the human race, can hardly be conceived, except where men have general rights (*jura communia*), and combine to defend the possession of the lands they inhabit and cultivate, to protect themselves, to repel all violence, and to live according to the general judgment of all. For (Sec. 13) the more there are that combine together, the more right they collectively possess. And if this is

why the schoolmen want to call man a sociable animal—I mean because men in the state of nature can hardly be independent—I have nothing to say against them.[5]

16. Where men have general rights, and are all guided, as it were, by one mind, it is certain (Sec. 13), that every individual has the less right the more the rest collectively exceed him in power; that is, he has, in fact, no right by nature but that which the common law allows him. But whatever he is ordered by the general consent, he is bound to execute, or may rightfully be compelled thereto (Sec. 4).

17. This right, which is determined by the power of a multitude, is generally called Dominion (*Imperium*). And, speaking generally, he holds dominion absolutely, to whom are entrusted by common consent affairs of state—such as the laying down, interpretation, and abrogation of laws, the fortification of cities, deciding on war and peace, &c. But if this charge belong to a council, composed of the general multitude, then the dominion is called a democracy (*Democratia*);[6] if the council be composed of certain chosen persons, then it is an aristocracy (*Aristocratia*); and if, lastly, the care of affairs of state and, consequently, the dominion rest with one man, then it has the name of monarchy (*Monarchia*).

18. From what we have proved in this chapter, it becomes clear to us that, in the state of nature, wrong-doing is impossible; or, if anyone does wrong, it is to himself, not to another.[7] For no one by the law of nature is bound to please another, unless he chooses, nor to hold anything to be good or evil, but what he himself, according to his own temperament, pronounces to be so; and, to speak generally, nothing is forbidden by the law of nature, except what is beyond everyone's power

[5] *Cf.* the selection from Ch. V of the *T. T.-P.,* above, pp. 24-26.
[6] *Cf.* Ch. XVI of the *T.T.-P.,* above, pp. 32-35.
[7] *Cf.* Ch. XVI of the *T.T.-P.,* above, pp. 27-32.

(Secs. 5 and 8). But wrongdoing is action, which cannot lawfully be committed. But if men by the ordinance of nature were bound to be led by reason, then all of necessity would be so led. For the ordinances (*instituta*) of nature are the ordinances of God (Secs. 2, 3), which God has instituted by the liberty, whereby he exists, and they follow, therefore, from the necessity of the divine nature (Sec. 7), and, consequently, are eternal, and cannot be broken. But men are chiefly guided by appetite, without reason; yet for all this they do not disturb the course of nature, but follow it of necessity. And, therefore, a man ignorant and weak of mind, is no more bound by natural law to order his life wisely, than a sick man is bound to be sound of body.

19. Therefore wrong-doing cannot be conceived of, but under dominion—that is, where, by the general right of the whole dominion (*Ex communi totius imperii jure*), it is decided what is good and what evil, and where no one does anything rightfully, save what he does in accordance with the general decree or consent (Sec. 16). For that, as we said in the last section, is wrong-doing, which cannot lawfully be committed, or is by law forbidden. But obedience is the constant will to execute that, which by law is good, and by the general decree ought to be done.[8]

20. Yet we are accustomed to call that also wrong, which is done against the sentence of sound reason, and to give the name of obedience to the constant will to moderate the appetite according to the dictate of reason: a manner of speech which I should quite approve, did human liberty consist in the licence of appetite, and slavery in the dominion of reason. But as human liberty is the greater, the more man can be guided by reason, and moderate his appetite, we cannot without great

[8] *Cf.* Ch. XVI of the *T. T.-P.,* above, pp. 34-35, and Ch. XIX, pp. 50-53.

impropriety call a rational life obedience, and give the name of wrong-doing to that which is, in fact, a weakness of the mind, not a licence of the mind directed against itself, and for which a man may be called a slave, rather than free (Secs. 7 and 11).

21. However, as reason teaches one to practise piety, and be of a calm and gentle spirit, which cannot be done save under dominion; and, further, as it is impossible for a multitude to be guided, as it were, by one mind, as under dominion is required, unless it has laws ordained according to the dictate of reason; men who are accustomed to live under dominion are not, therefore, using words so improperly, when they call that wrong-doing which is done against the sentence of reason, because the laws of the best dominion ought to be framed according to that dictate (Sec. 18). But, as for my saying (Sec. 18) that man in a state of nature, if he does wrong at all, does it against himself, see, on this point, Chap. IV., Secs. 4, 5, where is shown, in what sense we can say, that he who holds dominion and possesses natural right, is bound by laws and can do wrong.

22. As far as religion is concerned, it is further clear, that a man is most free and most obedient to himself when he most loves God, and worships him in sincerity. But so far as we regard, not the course of nature, which we do not understand, but the dictates of reason only, which respect religion, and likewise reflect that these dictates are revealed to us by God, speaking, as it were, within ourselves, or else were revealed to prophets as laws; so far, speaking in human fashion, we say that man obeys God when he worships him in sincerity, and, on the contrary, does wrong when he is led by blind desire. But, at the same time, we should remember that we are subject to God's power, as clay to that of the potter, who of the same lump makes some vessels unto honour, and others unto dishonour. And thus man can, indeed, act contrarily to the

decrees of God, as far as they have been written like laws in the minds of ourselves or the prophets, but against that eternal decree of God, which is written in universal nature, and has regard to the course of nature as a whole, he can do nothing.

23. As, then, wrong-doing and obedience, in their strict sense, so also justice and injustice cannot be conceived of, except under dominion. For nature offers nothing that can be called this man's rather than another's; but under nature everything belongs to all—that is, they have authority to claim it for themselves. But under dominion, where it is by common law determined what belongs to this man, and what to that, he is called just who has a constant will to render to every man his own, but he unjust who strives, on the contrary, to make his own that which belongs to another.

24. But that praise and blame are emotions of joy and sadness, accompanied by an idea of human excellence or weakness as their cause, we have explained in our Ethics.

CHAPTER III

OF THE RIGHT OF SUPREME AUTHORITIES [1]

UNDER every dominion the state is said to be Civil; but the entire body subject to a dominion is called a Commonwealth (*Civitas*) and the general business of the dominion, subject to the direction of him that holds it, has the name of Affairs of State (*Respublica*). Next we call men Citizens, as far as they enjoy by the civil law all the advantages of the commonwealth, and Subjects, as far as they are bound to obey its ordinances or laws. Lastly, we have already said that, of the civil state, there are three kinds—democracy, aristocracy, and monarchy (Chap. II. Sec. 17). Now, before I begin to treat of each kind separately, I will first deduce all the properties of the civil state (*status civilis*) in general. And of these, first of all comes to be considered the supreme right of the commonwealth, or the right of the supreme authorities.

2. From Chap. II. Sec. 15, it is clear that the right of the supreme authorities is nothing else than natural right itself, limited, indeed, by the power, not of every individual, but of the multitude, which is guided, as it were, by one mind—that is, as each individual in the state of nature, so the body and mind of a dominion have as much right as they have power. And thus each single citizen or subject has the less right, the more the commonwealth exceeds him in power (Chap. II. Sec. 16), and each citizen consequently does and has nothing, but what he may by the general decree of the commonwealth defend.

[1] *Cf.* Ch. XVI of the *T.T.-P.*, above.

3. If the commonwealth grant to any man the right, and therewith the authority (for else it is but a gift of words, Chap. II. Sec. 12) to live after his own mind, by that very act it abandons its own right, and transfers the same to him, to whom it has given such authority. But if it has given this authority to two or more, I mean authority to live each after his own mind, by that very act it has divided the dominion, and if, lastly, it has given this same authority to every citizen, it has thereby destroyed itself, and there remains no more a commonwealth, but everything returns to the state of nature; all of which is very manifest from what goes before. And thus it follows, that it can by no means be conceived, that every citizen should by the ordinance of the commonwealth live after his own mind, and accordingly this natural right of being one's own judge ceases in the civil state. I say expressly "by the ordinance of the commonwealth," for, if we weigh the matter aright, the natural right of every man does not cease in the civil state. For man, alike in the natural and in the civil state, acts according to the laws of his own nature, and consults his own interest. Man, I say, in each state is led by fear or hope to do or leave undone this or that; but the main difference between the two states is this, that in the civil state all fear the same things, and all have the same ground of security, and manner of life; and this certainly does not do away with the individual's faculty of judgment. For he that is minded to obey all the commonwealth's orders, whether through fear of its power or through love of quiet, certainly consults after his own heart his own safety and interest.

4. Moreover, we cannot even conceive, that every citizen should be allowed to interpret the commonwealth's decrees or laws. For were every citizen allowed this, he would thereby be his own judge, because each would easily be able to give a

colour of right to his own deeds, which by the last section
is absurd.

5. We see then, that every citizen depends not on himself,
but on the commonwealth, all whose commands he is bound to
execute, and has no right to decide, what is equitable or iniquitous, just or unjust. But, on the contrary, as the body of the
dominion should, so to speak, be guided by one mind, and
consequently the will of the commonwealth must be taken to
be the will of all; what the state decides to be just and good
must be held to be so decided by every individual. And so,
however iniquitous the subject may think the commonwealth's
decisions, he is none the less bound to execute them.[2]

6. But (it may be objected) is it not contrary to the dictate
of reason to subject one's self wholly to the judgment of another, and consequently, is not the civil state repugnant to
reason? Whence it would follow, that the civil state is irrational, and could only be created by men destitute of reason,
not at all by such as are led by it. But since reason teaches
nothing contrary to nature, sound reason cannot therefore dictate, that every one should remain independent, so long as men
are liable to passions (Chap. II. Sec. 15), that is, reason pronounces against such independence (Chap. I. Sec. 5). Besides,
reason altogether teaches to seek peace, and peace cannot be
maintained, unless the commonwealth's general laws be kept
unbroken. And so, the more a man is guided by reason, that is
(Chap. II. Sec. 11), the more he is free, the more constantly
he will keep the laws of the commonwealth, and execute the
commands of the supreme authority, whose subject he is. Furthermore, the civil state is naturally ordained to remove general fear, and prevent general sufferings, and therefore pursues
above everything the very end, after which everyone, who is led
by reason, strives, but in the natural state strives vainly (Chap.

2 *Cf.* the selection from Ch. XVII of the *T.T.-P.,* above, pp. 43-47.

II. Sec. 15). Wherefore, if a man who is led by reason, has sometimes to do by the commonwealth's order what he knows to be repugnant to reason, that harm is far compensated by the good, which he derives from the existence of a civil state. For it is reason's own law, to choose the less of two evils; and accordingly we may conclude, that no one is acting against the dictate of his own reason, so far as he does what by the law of the commonwealth is to be done. And this anyone will more easily grant us, after we have explained, how far the power and consequently the right of the commonwealth extends.

7. For, first of all, it must be considered, that, as in the state of nature the man who is led by reason is most powerful and most independent, so too that commonwealth will be most powerful and most independent, which is founded and guided by reason (Chapter II. Sec. 11). For the right of the commonwealth is determined by the power of the multitude, which is led, as it were, by one mind. But this unity of mind can in no wise be conceived, unless the commonwealth pursues chiefly the very end, which sound reason teaches is to the interest of all men.

8. In the second place it comes to be considered, that subjects are so far dependent not on themselves, but on the commonwealth, as they fear its power or threats, or as they love the civil state (Chap. II. Sec. 10). Whence it follows, that such things, as no one can be induced to do by rewards or threats, do not fall within the rights of the commonwealth. For instance, by reason of his faculty of judgment, it is in no man's power to believe.[3] For by what rewards or threats can a man be brought to believe, that the whole is not greater than its part, or that God does not exist, or that that is an infinite being, which he sees to be finite, or generally anything con-

---

[3] *Cf.* Ch. XX of the *T.T.-P.,* above.

trary to his sense or thought? So, too, by what rewards or threats can a man be brought to love one, whom he hates, or to hate one, whom he loves? And to this head must likewise be referred such things as are so abhorrent to human nature, that it regards them as actually worse than any evil, as that a man should be witness against himself, or torture himself, or kill his parents, or not strive to avoid death, and the like, to which no one can be induced by rewards or threats. But if we still choose to say, that the commonwealth has the right or authority to order such things, we can conceive of it in no other sense, than that in which one might say, that a man has the right to be mad or delirious. For what but a delirious fancy would such a right be, as could bind no one? And here I am speaking expressly of such things as cannot be subject to the right of a commonwealth and are abhorrent to human nature in general. For the fact, that a fool or madman can by no rewards or threats be induced to execute orders, or that this or that person, because he is attached to this or that religion, judges the laws of a dominion worse than any possible evil, in no wise makes void the laws of the commonwealth, since by them most of the citizens are restrained. And so, as those who are without fear or hope are so far independent (Chap. II. Sec. 10), they are, therefore, enemies of the dominion (Chap. II. Sec. 14), and may lawfully be coerced by force.

9. Thirdly and lastly, it comes to be considered, that those things are not so much within the commonwealth's right, which cause indignation in the majority. For it is certain, that by the guidance of nature men conspire together, either through common fear, or with the desire to avenge some common hurt; and as the right of the commonwealth is determined by the common power of the multitude, it is certain that the power and right of the commonwealth are so far diminished, as it gives occasion for many to conspire together. There are cer-

tainly some subjects of fear for a commonwealth, and as every separate citizen or in the state of nature every man, so a commonwealth is the less independent, the greater reason it has to fear. So much for the right of supreme authorities over subjects. Now before I treat of the right of the said authorities as against others, we had better resolve a question commonly mooted about religion.

10. For it may be objected to us, Do not the civil state, and the obedience of subjects, such as we have shown is required in the civil state, do away with religion, whereby we are bound to worship God? But if we consider the matter, as it really is, we shall find nothing that can suggest a scruple. For the mind, so far as it makes use of reason, is dependent, not on the supreme authorities, but on itself (Chap. II. Sec. 11). And so the true knowledge and the love of God cannot be subject to the dominion of any, nor yet can charity towards one's neighbour (Sec. 8). And if we further reflect, that the highest exercise of charity is that which aims at keeping peace and joining in unity, we shall not doubt that he does his duty, who helps everyone, so far as the commonwealth's laws, that is so far as unity and quiet allow. As for external rites, it is certain, that they can do no good or harm at all in respect of the true knowledge of God, and the love which necessarily results from it; and so they ought not to be held of such importance, that it should be thought worth while on their account to disturb public peace and quiet.[4] Moreover it is certain,

4 Spinoza everywhere maintains a fundamental distinction between the "outward observances of piety and the external rites of religion" on the one hand, and piety itself, "the inward worship of God" or "the means by which the mind is inwardly led to do homage to God in singleness of heart" on the other hand. Over the latter the sovereign can have no power and therefore no right. The following citation, from Ch. XIV of the *T. T.-P.*, may be collated with relevant passages in Chs. XVI, XIX, and XX printed above in this volume:

"As, then, each man's faith must be judged pious or impious only in

that I am not a champion of religion by the law of nature, that is (Chap. II. Sec. 3), by the divine decree. For I have no authority, as once the disciples of Christ had, to cast out unclean spirits and work miracles; which authority is yet so necessary to the propagating of religion in places where it is forbidden, that without it one not only, as they say, wastes one's time [5] and trouble, but causes besides very many inconveniences, whereof all ages have seen most mournful examples. Everyone therefore, wherever he may be, can worship God with true religion, and mind his own business, which is the duty of a private man. But the care of propagating religion should be left to God, or the supreme authorities, upon whom alone falls the charge of affairs of state. But I return to my subject.

11. After explaining the right of supreme authorities over citizens and the duty of subjects, it remains to consider the right of such authorities against the world at large, which is now easily intelligible from what has been said. For since (Sec. 2) the right of the supreme authorities is nothing else but natural right itself, it follows that two dominions stand towards each other in the same relation as do two men in the state of nature, with this exception, that a commonwealth can provide against being oppressed by another; which a man in the state of nature cannot do, seeing that he is overcome daily by sleep, often by disease or mental infirmity, and in the end

respect of its producing obedience or obstinacy, and not in respect of its truth; and as no one will dispute that men's dispositions are exceedingly varied, that all do not acquiesce in the same things ... it follows that there can be no doctrines in the catholic, or universal, religion, which can give rise to controversy among good men. ... To the universal religion, then, belong only such dogmas as are absolutely required in order to attain obedience to God, and without which such obedience would be impossible; as for the rest, each man ... should adopt whatever he thinks best adapted to strengthen his love of justice."

[5] Literally, "oil and trouble"—a common proverbial expression in Latin.

by old age, and is besides liable to other inconveniences, from which a commonwealth can secure itself.

12. A commonwealth then is so far independent, as it can plan and provide against oppression by another (Chap. II. Secs. 9, 15), and so far dependent on another commonwealth, as it fears that other's power, or is hindered by it from executing its own wishes, or lastly, as it needs its help for its own preservation or increase (Chap. II. Secs. 10, 15). For we cannot at all doubt, that if two commonwealths are willing to offer each other mutual help, both together are more powerful, and therefore have more right, than either alone (Chap. II. Sec. 13).

13. But this will be more clearly intelligible, if we reflect, that two commonwealths are naturally enemies. For men in the state of nature are enemies (Chap. II. Sec. 14). Those, then, who stand outside a commonwealth, and retain their natural rights, continue enemies. Accordingly, if one commonwealth wishes to make war on another and employ extreme measures to make that other dependent on itself, it may lawfully make the attempt, since it needs but the bare will of the commonwealth for war to be waged. But concerning peace it can decide nothing, save with the concurrence of another commonwealth's will. Whence it follows, that laws of war regard every commonwealth by itself, but laws of peace regard not one, but at the least two commonwealths, which are therefore called "contracting powers."

14. This "contract" (*fœdus*) remains so long unmoved as the motive for entering into it, that is, fear of hurt or hope of gain, subsists. But take away from either commonwealth this hope or fear, and it is left independent (Chap. II. Sec. 10), and the link, whereby the commonwealths were mutually bound, breaks of itself. And therefore every commonwealth has the right to break its contract, whenever it chooses, and

cannot be said to act treacherously or perfidiously in breaking its word, as soon as the motive of hope or fear is removed. For every contracting party was on equal terms in this respect, that whichever could first free itself of fear should be independent, and make use of its independence after its own mind; and, besides, no one makes a contract respecting the future, but on the hypothesis of certain precedent circumstances. But when these circumstances change, the reason of policy applicable to the whole position changes with them; and therefore every one of the contracting commonwealths retains the right of consulting its own interest, and consequently endeavours, as far as possible, to be free from fear and thereby independent, and to prevent another from coming out of the contract with greater power. If then a commonwealth complains that it has been deceived, it cannot properly blame the bad faith of another contracting commonwealth, but only its own folly in having entrusted its own welfare to another party, that was independent, and had for its highest law the welfare of its own dominion.

15. To commonwealths, which have contracted a treaty of peace, it belongs to decide the questions, which may be mooted about the terms or rules of peace, whereby they have mutually bound themselves, inasmuch as laws of peace regard not one commonwealth, but the commonwealths which contract taken together (Sec. 13). But if they cannot agree together about the conditions, they by that very fact return to a state of war.

16. The more commonwealths there are, that have contracted a joint treaty of peace, the less each of them by itself is an object of fear to the remainder, or the less it has the authority to make war. But it is so much the more bound to observe the conditions of peace; that is (Sec. 13), the less independent, and the more bound to accommodate itself to the general will of the contracting parties.

17. But the good faith, inculcated by sound reason and religion, is not hereby made void; for neither reason nor Scripture teaches one to keep one's word in every case. For if I have promised a man, for instance, to keep safe a sum of money he has secretly deposited with me, I am not bound to keep my word, from the time that I know or believe the deposit to have been stolen, but I shall act more rightly in endeavouring to restore it to its owners. So likewise, if the supreme authority has promised another to do something, which subsequently occasion or reason shows or seems to show is contrary to the welfare of its subjects, it is surely bound to break its word. As then Scripture only teaches us to keep our word in general, and leaves to every individual's judgment the special cases of exception, it teaches nothing repugnant to what we have just proved.

18. But that I may not have so often to break the thread of my discourse, and to resolve hereafter similar objections, I would have it known that all this demonstration of mine proceeds from the necessity of human nature, considered in what light you will—I mean, from the universal effort of all men after self-preservation, an effort inherent in all men, whether learned or unlearned. And therefore, however one considers men are led, whether by passion or by reason, it will be the same thing; for the demonstration, as we have said, is of universal application.

CHAPTER IV

OF THE FUNCTIONS OF SUPREME AUTHORITIES

THAT the right of the supreme authorities is limited by their power, we showed in the last chapter, and saw that the most important part of that right is, that they are, as it were, the mind of the dominion, whereby all ought to be guided; and accordingly, that such authorities alone have the right of deciding what is good, evil, equitable, or iniquitous, that is, what must be done or left undone by the subjects severally or collectively. And, accordingly, we saw that they have the sole right of laying down laws, and of interpreting the same, whenever their meaning is disputed, and of deciding whether a given case is in conformity with or violation of the law (Chap. III. Secs. 3-5); and, lastly, of waging war, and of drawing up and offering propositions for peace, or of accepting such when offered (Chap. III. Secs. 12, 13).

2. As all these functions, and also the means required to execute them, are matters which regard the whole body of the dominion, that is, are affairs of state, it follows, that affairs of state depend on the direction of him only, who holds supreme dominion. And hence it follows, that it is the right of the supreme authority alone to judge the deeds of every individual, and demand of him an account of the same; to punish criminals, and decide questions of law between citizens, or appoint jurists acquainted with the existing laws, to administer these matters on its behalf; and, further, to use and order all means to war and peace, as to found and fortify cities, levy soldiers, assign military posts, and order what it would have

done, and, with a view to peace, to send and give audience to ambassadors; and, finally, to levy the costs of all this.

3. Since, then, it is the right of the supreme authority alone to handle public matters, or choose officials to do so, it follows, that that subject is a pretender to the dominion, who, by his own decision and without the supreme council's knowledge, enters upon .any public matter, although he believe that his design will be to the best interest of the commonwealth.

4. But it is often asked, whether the supreme authority is bound by laws, and, consequently, whether it can do wrong. Now as the words "law" and "wrong-doing" often refer not merely to the laws of a commonwealth, but also to the general rules which concern all natural things, and especially to the general rules of reason, we cannot, without qualification, say that the commonwealth is bound by no laws, or can do no wrong. For were the commonwealth bound by no laws or rules, which removed, the commonwealth were no commonwealth, we should have to regard it not as a natural thing (*res naturalis*), but as a chimera. A commonwealth then does wrong, when it does, or suffers to be done, things which may be the cause of its own ruin; and we can say that it then does wrong, in the sense in which philosophers or doctors say that nature does wrong; and in this sense we can say, that a commonwealth does wrong, when it acts against the dictate of reason. For a commonwealth is most independent when it acts according to the dictate of reason (Chap. III. Sec. 7); so far, then, as it acts against reason, it fails itself, or does wrong. And we shall be able more easily to understand this if we reflect, that when we say, that a man can do what he will with his own, this authority must be limited not only by the power of the agent, but by the capacity of the object. If, for instance, I say that I can rightfully do what I will with this table, I do not certainly mean, that I have the right to make

it eat grass. So, too, though we say, that men depend not on themselves, but on the commonwealth, we do not mean, that men lose their human nature and put on another; nor yet that the commonwealth has the right to make men wish for this or that, or (what is just as impossible) regard with honour things which excite ridicule or disgust. But it is implied, that there are certain intervening circumstances, which supposed, one likewise supposes the reverence and fear of the subjects towards the commonwealth, and which abstracted, one makes abstraction likewise of that fear and reverence, and therewith of the commonwealth itself. The commonwealth, then, to maintain its independence, is bound to preserve the causes of fear and reverence, otherwise it ceases to be a commonwealth. For the person or persons that hold dominion, can no more combine with the keeping up of majesty the running with harlots drunk or naked about the streets, or the performances of a stage-player, or the open violation or contempt of laws passed by themselves, than they can combine existence with nonexistence. But to proceed to slay and rob subjects, ravish maidens, and the like, turns fear into indignation and the civil state into a state of enmity.

5. We see, then, in what sense we may say, that a commonwealth is bound by laws and can do wrong. But if by "law" we understand civil law, and by "wrong" that which, by civil law, is forbidden to be done, that is, if these words be taken in their proper sense, we cannot at all say, that a commonwealth is bound by laws, or can do wrong. For the maxims and motives of fear and reverence, which a commonwealth is bound to observe in its own interest, pertain not to civil jurisprudence, but to the law of nature, since (Sec. 4) they cannot be vindicated by the civil law, but by the law of war. And a commonwealth is bound by them in no other sense than that in which in the state of nature a man is bound to

take heed, that he preserve his independence and be not his own enemy, lest he should destroy himself; and in this taking heed lies not the subjection, but the liberty of human nature. But civil jurisprudence depends on the mere decree of the commonwealth, which is not bound to please any but itself, nor to hold anything to be good or bad, but what it judges to be such for itself. And, accordingly, it has not merely the right to avenge itself, or to lay down and interpret laws, but also to abolish the same, and to pardon any guilty person out of the fulness of its power.

6. Contracts or laws, whereby the multitude transfers its right to one council or man, should without doubt be broken, when it is expedient for the general welfare to do so. But to decide this point, whether, that is, it be expedient for the general welfare to break them or not, is within the right of no private person, but of him only who holds dominion (Sec. 3); therefore of these laws he who holds dominion remains sole interpreter. Moreover, no private person can by right vindicate these laws, and so they do not really bind him who holds dominion. Notwithstanding, if they are of such a nature that they cannot be broken, without at the same time weakening the commonwealth's strength, that is, without at the same time changing to indignation the common fear of most of the citizens, by this very fact the commonwealth is dissolved, and the contract comes to an end; and therefore such contract is vindicated not by the civil law, but by the law of war. And so he who holds dominion is not bound to observe the terms of the contract by any other cause than that, which bids a man in the state of nature to beware of being his own enemy, lest he should destroy himself, as we said in the last section.

Chapter V

Of the Best State of a Dominion

IN Chap. II. Sec. 2, we showed, that man is then most independent, when he is most led by reason, and, in consequence (Chap. III. Sec. 7), that that commonwealth is most powerful and most independent, which is founded and guided by reason. But, as the best plan of living, so as to assure to the utmost self-preservation, is that which is framed according to the dictate of reason, therefore it follows, that that in every kind is best done, which a man or commonwealth does, so far as he or it is in the highest degree independent. For it is one thing to till a field by right, and another to till it in the best way. One thing, I say, to defend or preserve one's self, and to pass judgment by right, and another to defend or preserve one's self in the best way, and to pass the best judgment; and, consequently, it is one thing to have dominion and care of affairs of state by right, and another to exercise dominion and direct affairs of state in the best way. And so, as we have treated of the right of every commonwealth in general, it is time to treat of the best state of every dominion.[1]

2. Now the quality of the state of any dominion is easily perceived from the end of the civil state, which end is nothing else but peace and security of life. And therefore that dominion is the best, where men pass their lives in unity, and the laws are kept unbroken. For it is certain, that seditions, wars, and contempt or breach of the laws are not so much

[1] *Cf.* the selection from Ch. XVII of the *T. T.-P.,* above, pp. 43-47.

to be imputed to the wickedness of the subjects, as to the bad state of a dominion. For men are not born fit for citizenship, but must be made so. Besides, men's natural passions are everywhere the same; and if wickedness more prevails, and more offences are committed in one commonwealth than in another, it is certain that the former has not enough pursued the end of unity, nor framed its laws with sufficient forethought; and that, therefore, it has failed in making quite good its right as a commonwealth. For a civil state, which has not done away with the causes of seditions, where war is a perpetual object of fear, and where, lastly, the laws are often broken, differs but little from the mere state of nature, in which everyone lives after his own mind at the great risk of his life.

3. But as the vices and inordinate licence and contumacy of subjects must be imputed to the commonwealth, so, on the other hand, their virtue and constant obedience to the laws are to be ascribed in the main to the virtue and perfect right of the commonwealth, as is clear from Chap. II. Sec. 15. And so it is deservedly reckoned to Hannibal as an extraordinary virtue, that in his army there never arose a sedition.

4. Of a commonwealth, whose subjects are but hindered by terror from taking arms, it should rather be said, that it is free from war, than that it has peace. For peace is not mere absence of war, but is a virtue that springs from force of character: for obedience (Chap. II. Sec. 19) is the constant will to execute what, by the general decree of the commonwealth, ought to be done. Besides, that commonwealth, whose peace depends on the sluggishness of its subjects, that are led about like sheep, to learn but slavery, may more properly be called a desert than a commonwealth.

5. When, then, we call that dominion best, where men pass their lives in unity, I understand a human life, defined not by mere circulation of the blood, and other qualities common to

all animals, but above all by reason, the true excellence and life of the mind.

6. But be it remarked that, by the dominion which I have said is established for this end, I intend that which has been established by a free multitude, not that which is acquired over a multitude by right of war. For a free multitude is guided more by hope than fear; a conquered one, more by fear than hope: inasmuch as the former aims at making use of life, the latter but at escaping death. The former, I say, aims at living for its own ends, the latter is forced to belong to the conqueror; and so we say that this is enslaved, but that free. And, therefore, the end of a dominion, which one gets by right of war, is to be master, and have rather slaves than subjects. And although between the dominion created by a free multitude, and that gained by right of war, if we regard generally the right of each, we can make no essential distinction; yet their ends, as we have already shown, and further the means to the preservation of each are very different.

7. But what means a prince, whose sole motive is lust of mastery, should use to establish and maintain his dominion, the most ingenious Machiavelli has set forth at large, but with what design one can hardly be sure. If, however, he had some good design, as one should believe of a learned man, it seems to have been to show, with how little foresight many attempt to remove a tyrant, though thereby the causes which make the prince a tyrant can in no wise be removed, but, on the contrary, are so much the more established, as the prince is given more cause to fear, which happens when the multitude has made an example of its prince, and glories in the parricide as in a thing well done. Moreover, he perhaps wished to show how cautious a free multitude should be of entrusting its welfare absolutely to one man, who, unless in his vanity he thinks he can please everybody, must be in daily fear of plots, and

so is forced to look chiefly after his own interest, and, as for the multitude, rather to plot against it than consult its good. And I am the more led to this opinion concerning that most far-seeing man, because it is known that he was favourable to liberty, for the maintenance of which he has besides given the most wholesome advice.

Chapter VI

Of Monarchy

INASMUCH as men are led, as we have said, more by passion than reason, it follows, that a multitude comes together, and wishes to be guided, as it were, by one mind, not at the suggestion of reason, but of some common passion— that is (Chap. III. Sec. 9), common hope, or fear, or the desire of avenging some common hurt. But since fear of solitude exists in all men, because no one in solitude is strong enough to defend himself, and procure the necessaries of life, it follows that men naturally aspire to the civil state; nor can it happen that men should ever utterly dissolve it.

2. Accordingly, from the quarrels and seditions which are often stirred up in a commonwealth, it never results that the citizens dissolve it, as often happens in the case of other associations; but only that they change its form into some other— that is, of course, if the disputes cannot be settled, and the features of the commonwealth at the same time preserved. Wherefore, by means necessary to preserve a dominion, I intend such things as are necessary to preserve the existing form of the dominion, without any notable change.

3. But if human nature were so constituted, that men most desired what is most useful, no art would be needed to produce unity and confidence. But, as it is admittedly far otherwise with human nature, a dominion must of necessity be so ordered, that all, governing and governed alike, whether they will or no, shall do what makes for the general welfare; that is, that all, whether of their own impulse, or by force or

necessity, shall be compelled to live according to the dictate of reason. And this is the case, if the affairs of the dominion be so managed, that nothing which affects the general welfare is entirely entrusted to the good faith of any one. For no man is so watchful, that he never falls asleep; and no man ever had a character so vigorous and honest, but he sometimes, and that just when strength of character was most wanted, was diverted from his purpose and let himself be overcome. And it is surely folly to require of another what one can never obtain from one's self; I mean, that he should be more watchful for another's interest than his own, that he should be free from avarice, envy, and ambition, and so on; especially when he is one, who is subject daily to the strongest temptations of every passion.

4. But, on the other hand, experience is thought to teach, that it makes for peace and concord, to confer the whole authority upon one man. For no dominion has stood so long without any notable change, as that of the Turks, and on the other hand there were none so little lasting, as those, which were popular or democratic, nor any in which so many seditions arose. Yet if slavery, barbarism, and desolation are to be called peace, men can have no worse misfortune. No doubt there are usually more and sharper quarrels between parents and children, than between masters and slaves; yet it advances not the art of housekeeping, to change a father's right into a right of property, and count children but as slaves. Slavery then, not peace, is furthered by handing over to one man the whole authority. For peace, as we said before, consists not in mere absence of war, but in a union or agreement of minds.

5. And in fact they are much mistaken, who suppose that one man *can* by himself hold the supreme right of a commonwealth. For the only limit of right, as we showed (Chap. II.), is power. But the power of one man is very inadequate to

support so great a load. And hence it arises, that the man, whom the multitude has chosen king, looks out for himself generals, or counsellors, or friends, to whom he entrusts his own and the common welfare; so that the dominion, which is thought to be a perfect monarchy, is in actual working an aristocracy, not, indeed, an open but a hidden one, and therefore the worst of all. Besides which, a king, who is a boy, or ill, or overcome by age, is but king on sufferance; and those in this case have the supreme authority, who administer the highest business of the dominion, or are near the king's person; not to mention, that a lascivious king often manages everything at the caprice of this or that mistress or minion. "I had heard," says Orsines, "that women once reigned in Asia, but for a eunuch to reign is something new."

6. It is also certain, that a commonwealth is always in greater danger from its citizens than from its enemies; for the good are few. Whence it follows, that he, upon whom the whole right of the dominion has been conferred, will always be more afraid of citizens than of enemies, and therefore will look to his own safety, and not try to consult his subjects' interests, but to plot against them, especially against those who are renowned for learning, or have influence through wealth.

7. It must besides be added, that kings fear their sons also more than they love them, and so much the more as the latter are skilled in the arts of war and peace, and endeared to the subjects by their virtues. Whence it comes, that kings try so to educate their sons, that they may have no reason to fear them. Wherein ministers very readily obey the king, and will be at the utmost pains, that the successor may be an inexperienced king, whom they can hold tightly in hand.

8. From all which it follows, that the more absolutely the commonwealth's right is transferred to the king, the less independent he is, and the more unhappy is the condition of his

subjects. And so, that a monarchical dominion may be duly established, it is necessary to lay solid foundations, to build it on; from which may result to the monarch safety, and to the multitude peace; and, therefore, to lay them in such a way, that the monarch may then be most independent, when he most consults the multitude's welfare. But I will first briefly state, what these foundations of a monarchical dominion are, and afterwards prove them in order.

9. One or more cities must be founded and fortified, whose citizens, whether they live within the walls, or outside for purposes of agriculture, are all to enjoy the same right in the commonwealth; yet on this condition, that every city provide an ascertained number of citizens for its own and the general defence. But a city, which cannot supply this, must be held in subjection on other terms.

10. The militia must be formed out of citizens alone, none being exempt, and of no others. And, therefore, all are to be bound to have arms, and no one to be admitted into the number of the citizens, till he has learnt his drill, and promised to practise it at stated times in the year. Next, the militia of each clan is to be divided into battalions and regiments, and no captain of a battalion chosen, that is not acquainted with military engineering. Moreover, though the commanders of battalions and regiments are to be chosen for life, yet the commander of the militia of a whole clan is to be chosen only in time of war, to hold command for a year at most, without power of being continued or afterwards re-appointed. And these last are to be selected out of the king's counsellors, of whom we shall speak in the fifteenth and following sections, or out of those who have filled the post of counsellor.

11. The townsmen and countrymen of every city, that is, the whole of the citizens, are to be divided into clans, distinguished by some name and badge, and all persons born of

any of these clans are to be received into the number of citizens, and their names inscribed on the roll of their clan, as soon as they have reached the age, when they can carry arms and know their duty; with the exception of those, who are infamous from some crime, or dumb, or mad, or menials supporting life by some servile office.

12. The fields, and the whole soil, and, if it can be managed, the houses should be public property, that is, the property of him, who holds the right of the commonwealth: and let him let them at a yearly rent to the citizens, whether townsmen or countrymen, and with this exception let them all be free or exempt from every kind of taxation in time of peace. And of this rent a part is to be applied to the defences of the state, a part to the king's private use. For it is necessary in time of peace to fortify cities against war, and also to have ready ships and other munitions of war.

13. After the selection of the king from one of the clans, none are to be held noble, but his descendants, who are therefore to be distinguished by royal insignia from their own and the other clans.

14. Those male nobles, who are the reigning king's collaterals, and stand to him in the third or fourth degree of consanguinity, must not marry, and any children they may have had, are to be accounted bastards, and unworthy of any dignity, nor may they be recognized as heirs to their parents, whose goods must revert to the king.

15. Moreover the king's counsellors, who are next to him in dignity, must be numerous, and chosen out of the citizens only; that is (supposing there to be no more than six hundred clans) from every clan three or four or five, who will form together one section of this council; and not for life, but for three, four, or five years, so that every year a third, fourth, or fifth part may be replaced by selection, in which selection it must be

observed as a first condition, that out of every clan at least one counsellor chosen be a jurist.

16. The selection must be made by the king himself, who should fix a time of year for the choice of fresh counsellors. Each clan must then submit to the king the names of all its citizens, who have reached their fiftieth year, and have been duly put forward as candidates for this office, and out of these the king will choose whom he pleases. But in that year, when the jurist of any clan is to be replaced, only the names of jurists are to be submitted to the king. Those who have filled this office of counsellor for the appointed time, are not to be continued therein, nor to be replaced on the list of candidates for five years or more. But the reason why one is to be chosen every year out of every clan is, that the council may not be composed alternately of untried novices, and of veterans versed in affairs, which must necessarily be the case, were all to retire at once, and new men to succeed them. But if every year one be chosen out of every family, then only a fifth, fourth, or at most a third part of the council will consist of novices. Further, if the king be prevented by other business, or for any other reason, from being able to spare time for this choice, then let the counsellors themselves choose others for a time, until the king either chooses different ones, or confirms the choice of the council.

17. Let the primary function of this council be to defend the fundamental laws of the dominion, and to give advice about administration, that the king may know, what for the public good ought to be decreed: and that on the understanding, that the king may not decide in any matter, without first hearing the opinion of this council. But if, as will generally happen, the council is not of one mind, but is divided in opinion, even after discussing the same subject two or three times, there must be no further delay, but the different opinions are

to be submitted to the king, as in the twenty-fifth section of this chapter we shall show.

18. Let it be also the duty of this council to publish the king's orders or decrees, and to see to the execution of any decree concerning affairs of state, and to supervise the administration of the whole dominion, as the king's deputies.

19. The citizens should have no access to the king, save through this council, to which are to be handed all demands or petitions, that they may be presented to the king. Nor should the envoys of other commonwealths be allowed to obtain permission to address the king, but through the council. Letters, too, sent from elsewhere to the king, must be handed to him by the council. And in general the king is to be accounted as the mind of the commonwealth, but the council as the senses outside the mind, or the commonwealth's body, through whose intervention the mind understands the state of the commonwealth, and acts as it judges best for itself.

20. The care of the education of the king's sons should also fall on this council, and the guardianship, where a king has died, leaving as his successor an infant or boy. Yet lest meanwhile the council should be left without a king, one of the elder nobles of the commonwealth should be chosen to fill the king's place, till the legitimate heir has reached the age at which he can support the weight of government.

21. Let the candidates for election to this council be such as know the system of government, and the foundations, and state or condition of the commonwealth, whose subjects they are. But he that would fill the place of a jurist must, besides the government and condition of the commonwealth, whose subject he is, be likewise acquainted with those of the other commonwealths, with which it has any intercourse. But none are to be placed upon the list of candidates, unless they have reached their fiftieth year without being convicted of crime.

22. In this council no decision is to be taken about the affairs of the dominion, but in the presence of all the members. But if anyone be unable through illness or other cause to attend, he must send in his stead one of the same clan, who has filled the office of counsellor or been put on the list of candidates. Which if he neglect to do, and the council through his absence be forced to adjourn any matter, let him be fined a considerable sum. But this must be understood to mean, when the question is of a matter affecting the whole dominion, as of peace or war, of abrogating or establishing a law, of trade, &c. But if the question be one that affects only a particular city or two, as about petitions, &c., it will suffice that a majority of the council attend.

23. To maintain a perfect equality between the clans, and a regular order in sitting, making proposals, and speaking, every clan is to take in turn the presidency at the sittings, a different clan at every sitting, and that which was first at one sitting is to be last at the next. But among members of the same clan, let precedence go by priority of election.

24. This council should be summoned at least four times a year, to demand of the ministers account of their administration of the dominion, to ascertain the state of affairs, and see if anything else needs deciding. For it seems impossible for so large a number of citizens to have constant leisure for public business. But as in the meantime public business must none the less be carried on, therefore fifty or more are to be chosen out of this council to supply its place after its dismissal; and these should meet daily in a chamber next the king's, and so have daily care of the treasury, the cities, the fortifications, the education of the king's son, and in general of all those duties of the great council, which we have just enumerated, except that they cannot take counsel about new matters, concerning which no decision has been taken.

25. On the meeting of the council, before anything is proposed in it, let five, six, or more jurists of the clans, which
stand first in order of place at that session, attend on the king,
to deliver to him petitions or letters, if they have any, to declare
to him the state of affairs, and, lastly, to understand from him
what he bids them propose in his council; and when they have
heard this, let them return to the council, and let the first in
precedence open the matter of debate. But, in matters which
seem to any of them to be of some moment, let not the votes
be taken at once, but let the voting be adjourned to such a date
as the urgency of the matter allows. When, then, the council
stands adjourned till the appointed time, the counsellors of
every clan will meanwhile be able to debate the matter separately, and, if they think it of great moment, to consult others
that have been counsellors, or are candidates for the council.
And if within the appointed time the counsellors of any clan
cannot agree among themselves, that clan shall lose its vote,
for every clan can give but one vote. But, otherwise, let the
jurist of the clan lay before the council the opinion they have
decided to be best; and so with the rest. And if the majority
of the council think fit, after hearing the grounds of every
opinion, to consider the matter again, let the council be again
adjourned to a date, at which every clan shall pronounce its
final opinion; and then, at last, before the entire council, let
the votes be taken, and that opinion be invalidated which has
not at least a hundred votes. But let the other opinions be
submitted to the king by all the jurists present at the council,
that, after hearing every party's arguments, he may select which
opinion he pleases. And then let the jurists leave him, and
return to the council; and there let all await the king at the
time fixed by himself, that all may hear which opinion of those
proposed he thinks fit to adopt, and what he decides should
be done.

26. For the administration of justice, another council is to be formed of jurists, whose business should be to decide suits, and punish criminals, but so that all the judgments they deliver be tested by those who are for the time members of the great council—that is, as to their having been delivered according to the due process of justice, and without partiality. But if the losing party can prove, that any judge has been bribed by the adversary, or that there is some mutual cause of friendship between the judge and the adversary, or of hatred between the judge and himself, or, lastly, that the usual process of justice has not been observed, let such party be restored to his original position. But this would, perhaps, not be observed by such as love to convict the accused in a criminal case, rather by torture than proofs. But, for all that, I can conceive on this point of no other process of justice than the above, that befits the best system of governing the commonwealth.

27. Of these judges, there should be a large and odd number —for instance, sixty-one, or at least forty-one,—and not more than one is to be chosen of one clan, and that not for life, but every year a certain portion are to retire, and be replaced by as many others out of different clans, that have reached their fortieth year.

28. In this council, let no judgment be pronounced save in the presence of all the judges. But if any judge, from disease or other cause, shall for a long time be unable to attend the council, let another be chosen for that time to fill his place. But in giving their votes, they are all not to utter their opinions aloud, but to signify them by ballot.

29. Let those who supply others' places in this and the first-mentioned council first be paid out of the goods of those whom they have condemned to death, and also out of the fines of which any are mulcted. Next, after every judgment they pro-

nounce in a civil suit, let them receive a certain proportion of the whole sum at stake for the benefit of both councils.

30. Let there be in every city other subordinate councils, whose members likewise must not be chosen for life, but must be partially renewed every year, out of the clans who live there only. But there is no need to pursue this further.

31. No military pay is to be granted in time of peace; but, in time of war, military pay is to be allowed to those only, who support their lives by daily labour. But the commanders and other officers of the battalions are to expect no other advantage from war but the spoil of the enemy.

32. If a foreigner takes to wife the daughter of a citizen, his children are to be counted citizens, and put on the roll of their mother's clan. But those who are born and bred within the dominion of foreign parents should be allowed to purchase at a fixed price the right of citizenship from the captains of thousands of any clan, and to be enrolled in that clan. For no harm can arise thence to the dominion, even though the captains of thousands, for a bribe, admit a foreigner into the number of their citizens for less than the fixed price; but, on the contrary, means should be devised for more easily increasing the number of citizens, and producing a large confluence of men. As for those who are not enrolled as citizens, it is but fair that, at least in war-time, they should pay for their exemption from service by some forced labour or tax.

33. The envoys to be sent in time of peace to other commonwealths must be chosen out of the nobles only, and their expenses met by the state treasury, and not the king's privy purse.

34. Those that attend the court, and are the king's servants, and are paid out of his privy purse, must be excluded from every appointment and office in the commonwealth. I say expressly, "and are paid out of the king's privy purse," to

except the body-guard. For there should be no other body-guard, but the citizens of the king's city, who should take turns to keep guard at court before the king's door.

35. War is only to be made for the sake of peace, so that, at its end, one may be rid of arms. And so, when cities have been taken by right of war, and terms of peace are to be made after the enemies are subdued, the captured cities must not be garrisoned and kept; but either the enemy, on accepting the terms of peace, should be allowed to redeem them at a price, or, if by following that policy, there would, by reason of the danger of the position, remain a constant lurking anxiety, they must be utterly destroyed, and the inhabitants removed elsewhere.

36. The king must not be allowed to contract a foreign marriage, but only to take to wife one of his kindred, or of the citizens; yet, on condition that, if he marries a citizen, her near relations become incapable of holding office in the commonwealth.

37. The dominion must be indivisible. And so, if the king leaves more than one child, let the eldest one succeed; but by no means be it allowed to divide the dominion between them, or to give it undivided to all or several of them, much less to give a part of it as a daughter's dowry. For that daughters should be admitted to the inheritance of a dominion is in no wise to be allowed.

38. If the king die leaving no male issue, let the next to him in blood be held the heir to the dominion, unless he chance to have married a foreign wife, whom he will not put away.

39. As for the citizens, it is manifest (Chap. III. Sec. 5) that every one of them ought to obey all the commands of the king, and the decrees published by the great council, although he believe them to be most absurd, and otherwise he may rightfully be forced to obey. And these are the founda-

tions of a monarchical dominion, on which it must be built, if it is to be stable, as we shall show in the next chapter.

40. As for religion, no temples whatever ought to be built at the public expense; nor ought laws to be established about opinions, unless they be seditious and overthrow the foundations of the commonwealth. And so let such as are allowed the public exercise of their religion build a temple at their own expense. But the king may have in his palace a chapel of his own, that he may practise the religion to which he belongs.

CHAPTER VII

OF MONARCHY. PROOF OF THE FOUNDATIONS OF A MONARCHICAL DOMINION

AFTER explaining the foundations of a monarchical dominion, I have taken in hand to prove here in order the
fitness of such foundations. And to this end the first point to
be noted is, that it is in no way repugnant to experience, for
laws to be so firmly fixed, that not the king himself can abolish
them. For though the Persians worshipped their kings as gods,
yet had not the kings themselves authority to revoke laws once
established, as appears from Daniel, and nowhere, as far as I
know, is a monarch chosen absolutely without any conditions
expressed. Nor yet is it repugnant to reason or the absolute
obedience due to a king. For the foundations of the dominion
are to be considered as eternal decrees of the king, so that his
ministers entirely obey him in refusing to execute his orders,
when he commands anything contrary to the same. Which
we can make plain by the example of Ulysses. For his comrades
were executing his own order, when they would not untie him,
when he was bound to the mast and captivated by the Sirens'
song, although he gave them manifold orders to do so, and
that with threats. And it is ascribed to his forethought, that
he afterwards thanked his comrades for obeying him according
to his first intention. And, after this example of Ulysses, kings
often instruct judges, to administer justice without respect of
persons, not even of the king himself, if by some singular
accident he order anything contrary to established law. For
kings are not gods, but men, who are often led captive by the

127

Sirens' song. If then everything depended on the inconstant will of one man, nothing would be fixed. And so, that a monarchical dominion may be stable, it must be ordered, so that everything be done by the king's decree only, that is, so that every law be an explicit will of the king, but not every will of the king a law; as to which see Chap. VI. Sects. 3, 5, 6.

2. It must next be observed, that in laying foundations it is very necessary to study the human passions: and it is not enough to have shown, what ought to be done, but it ought, above all, to be shown how it can be effected, that men, whether led by passion or reason, should yet keep the laws firm and unbroken. For if the constitution of the dominion, or the public liberty depends only on the weak assistance of the laws, not only will the citizens have no security for its maintenance (as we showed in the third section of the last chapter), but it will even turn to their ruin. For this is certain, that no condition of a commonwealth is more wretched than that of the best, when it begins to totter, unless at one blow it falls with a rush into slavery, which seems to be quite impossible. And, therefore, it would be far better for the subjects to transfer their rights absolutely to one man, than to bargain for unascertained and empty, that is unmeaning, terms of liberty, and so prepare for their posterity a way to the most cruel servitude. But if I succeed in showing that the foundations of monarchical dominion, which I stated in the last chapter, are firm and cannot be plucked up, without the indignation of the larger part of an armed multitude, and that from them follow peace and security for king and multitude, and if I deduce this from general human nature, no one will be able to doubt, that these foundations are the best and the true ones (Chap. III. Sec. 9, and Chap. VI. Sects. 3, 8). But that such is their nature, I will show as briefly as possible.

3. That the duty of him, who holds the dominion, is always

to know its state and condition, to watch over the common welfare of all, and to execute whatever is to the interest of the majority of the subjects, is admitted by all. But as one person alone is unable to examine into everything, and cannot always have his mind ready and turn it to meditation, and is often hindered by disease, or old age, or other causes, from having leisure for public business; therefore it is necessary that the monarch have counsellors to know the state of affairs, and help the king with their advice, and frequently supply his place; and that so it come to pass, that the dominion or commonwealth may continue always in one and the same mind.

4. But as human nature is so constituted, that everyone seeks with the utmost passion his own advantage, and judges those laws to be most equitable, which he thinks necessary to preserve and increase his substance, and defends another's cause so far only as he thinks he is thereby establishing his own; it follows hence, that the counsellors chosen must be such, that their private affairs and their own interests depend on the general welfare and peace of all. And so it is evident, that if from every sort or class of citizens a certain number be chosen, what has most votes in such a council will be to the interest of the greater part of the subjects. And though this council, because it is composed of so large a number of citizens, must of necessity be attended by many of very simple intellect, yet this is certain, that everyone is pretty clever and sagacious in business which he has long and eagerly practised. And, therefore, if none be chosen but such as have till their fiftieth year practised their own business without disgrace, they will be fit enough to give their advice about their own affairs, especially if, in matters of considerable importance, a time be allowed for consideration. Besides, it is far from being the fact, that a council composed of a few is not frequented by this kind of men. For, on the

contrary, its greatest part must consist of such, since everyone, in that case, tries hard to have dullards for colleagues, that they may hang on his words, for which there is no opportunity in large councils.

5. Furthermore, it is certain, that everyone would rather rule than be ruled. "For no one of his own will yields up dominion to another," as Sallust has it in his first speech to Cæsar. And, therefore, it is clear, that a whole multitude will never transfer its right to a few or to one, if it can come to an agreement with itself, without proceeding from the controversies, which generally arise in large councils, to seditions. And so the multitude does not, if it is free, transfer to the king anything but that, which it cannot itself have absolutely within its authority, namely, the ending of controversies and the using despatch in decisions. For as to the case which often arises, where a king is chosen on account of war, that is, because war is much more happily conducted by kings, it is manifest folly, I say, that men should choose slavery in time of peace for the sake of better fortune in war; if, indeed, peace can be conceived of in a dominion, where merely for the sake of war the highest authority is transferred to one man, who is, therefore, best able to show his worth and the importance to everyone of his single self in time of war; whereas, on the contrary, democracy has this advantage, that its excellence is greater in peace than in war. However, for whatever reason a king is chosen, he cannot by himself, as we said just now, know what will be to the interest of the dominion: but for this purpose, as we showed in the last section, will need many citizens for his counsellors. And as we cannot at all suppose, that any opinion can be conceived about a matter proposed for discussion, which can have escaped the notice of so large a number of men, it follows, that no opinion can be conceived tending to the people's welfare, besides all the opinions of this

council, which are submitted to the king. And so, since the people's welfare is the highest law, or the king's utmost right, it follows, that the king's utmost right is but to choose one of the opinions offered by the council, not to decree anything, or offer any opinion contrary to the mind of all the council at once (Chap. VI. Sec. 25). But if all the opinions offered in the council were to be submitted to the king, then it might happen that the king would always favour the small cities, which have the fewest votes. For though by the constitution of the council it be ordained, that the opinions should be submitted to the king without mention of their support-ers, yet they will never be able to take such good care, but that some opinion will get divulged. And, therefore, it must of necessity be provided, that that opinion, which has not gained at least a hundred votes, shall be held void; and this law the larger cities will be sure to defend with all their might.

6. And here, did I not study brevity, I would show other advantages of this council; yet one, which seems of the greatest importance, I will allege. I mean, that there can be given no greater inducement to virtue, than this general hope of the highest honour. For by ambition are we all most led, as in our Ethics we showed to be the case.[1]

7. But it cannot be doubted that the majority of this council will never be minded to wage war, but rather always pursue and love peace. For besides that war will always cause them fear of losing their property and liberty, it is to be added, that war requires fresh expenditure, which they must meet, and also that their own children and relatives, though intent on their domestic cares, will be forced to turn their attention to war and go a-soldiering, whence they will never bring back anything but unpaid-for scars. For, as we said (Chap. VI. Sec. 31), no

[1] Ethics, iii. 29, 30; IV. 58.

pay is to be given to the militia, and (Chap. VI. Sec. 10) it is to be formed out of citizens only and no others.

8. There is another accession to the cause of peace and concord, which is also of great weight: I mean, that no citizen can have immovable property (Chap. VI. Sec. 12). Hence all will have nearly an equal risk in war. For all will be obliged, for the sake of gain, to practise trade, or lend money to one another, if, as formerly by the Athenians, a law be passed, forbidding to lend money at interest to any but inhabitants; and thus they will be engaged in business, which either is mutually involved, one man's with another's, or needs the same means for its furtherance. And thus the greatest part of this council will generally have one and the same mind about their common affairs and the arts of peace. For, as we said (Sec. 4), every man defends another's cause, so far as he thinks thereby to establish his own.

9. It cannot be doubted, that it will never occur to anyone to corrupt this council with bribes. For were any man to draw over to his side some one or two out of so great a number of men, he would gain nothing. For, as we said, the opinion, which does not gain at least a hundred votes, is void.

10. We shall also easily see, that, once this council is established its members cannot be reduced to a less number, if we consider the common passions of mankind. For all are guided mostly by ambition, and there is no man who lives in health but hopes to attain extreme old age. If then we calculate the number of those who actually reach their fiftieth or sixtieth year, and further take into account the number that are every year chosen of this great council, we shall see, that there can hardly be a man of those who bear arms, but is under the influence of a great hope of attaining this dignity. And so they will all, to the best of their power, defend this law of the council. For be it noted, that corruption, unless it creep in

gradually, is easily prevented. But as it can be more easily supposed, and would be less invidious, that a less number should
be chosen out of every clan, than that a less number should be
chosen out of a few clans, or that one or two clans should
be altogether excluded; therefore (Chap. VI. Sec. 15) the number of counsellors cannot be reduced, unless a third, fourth, or
fifth part be removed simultaneously, which change is a very
great one, and therefore quite repugnant to common practice.
Nor need one be afraid of delay or negligence in choosing,
because this is remedied by the council itself. See Chap. VI.
Sec. 16.

11. The king, then, whether he is induced by fear of the
multitude, or aims at binding to himself the majority of an
armed multitude, or is guided by a generous spirit, a wish that
is, to consult the public interest, will always confirm that opinion, which has gained most votes, that is (Sec. 5), which is to
the interest of the greater part of the dominion, and will study
to reconcile the divergent opinions referred to him, if it can
be done, that he may attach all to himself (in which he will
exert all his powers), and that alike in peace and war they
may find out, what an advantage his single self is to them.
And thus he will then be most independent, and most in possession of dominion, when he most consults the general welfare of the multitude.

12. For the king by himself cannot restrain all by fear. But
his power, as we have said, rests upon the number of his
soldiers, and especially on their valour and faith, which will
always remain so long enduring between men, as with them
is joined need, be that need honourable or disgraceful. And
this is why kings usually are fonder of exciting than restrain-
ing their soldiery, and shut their eyes more to their vices than
to their virtues, and generally, to hold under the best of them,
seek out, distinguish, and assist with money or favour the idle,

and those who have ruined themselves by debauchery, and shake hands with them, and throw them kisses, and for the sake of mastery stoop to every servile action. In order therefore that the citizens may be distinguished by the king before all others, and, as far as the civil state and equity permit, may remain independent, it is necessary that the militia should consist of citizens only, and that citizens should be his counsellors; and on the contrary citizens are altogether subdued, and are laying the foundations of eternal war, from the moment that they suffer mercenaries to be levied, whose trade is war, and who have most power in strifes and seditions.

13. That the king's counsellors ought not to be elected for life, but for three, four, or five years, is clear as well from the tenth, as from what we said in the ninth section of this chapter. For if they were chosen for life, not only could the greatest part of the citizens conceive hardly any hope of obtaining this honour, and thus there would arise a great inequality, and thence envy, and constant murmurs, and at last seditions, which, no doubt, would be welcome to kings greedy of mastery: but also the counsellors, being rid of the fear of their successors, would assume a great licence in all respects, which the king would be far from opposing. For the more the citizens hate them, the more they will cling to the king, and be ready to flatter him. Nay, the interval of five years seems even too much, for in such a space of time it does not seem so impossible to corrupt by bribes or favour a very large part of the council, however large it be. And therefore it will be far safer, if every year two out of every clan retire, and be replaced by as many more (supposing that there are to be five counsellors of each clan), except in the year in which the jurist of any clan retires, and a fresh one is chosen in his place.

14. Moreover, no king can promise himself more safety, than he who reigns in a commonwealth of this sort. For besides

that a king soon perishes, when his soldiers cease to desire his safety, it is certain that kings are always in the greatest danger from those who are nearest their persons. The fewer counsellors, then, there are, and the more powerful they consequently are, the more the king is in danger of their transferring the dominion to another. Nothing in fact more alarmed David, than that his own counsellor Ahitophel sided with Absalom. Still more is this the case, if the whole authority has been transferred absolutely to one man, because it can then be more easily transferred from one to another. For two private soldiers once took in hand to transfer the Roman empire, and did transfer it. I omit the arts and cunning wiles, whereby counsellors have to assure themselves against falling victims to their unpopularity; for they are but too well known, and no one, who has read history, can be ignorant, that the good faith of counsellors has generally turned to their ruin. And so, for their own safety, it behoves them to be cunning, not faithful. But if the counsellors are too numerous to unite in the same crime, and are all equal, and do not hold their office beyond a period of four years, they cannot be at all objects of fear to the king, except he attempt to take away their liberty, wherein he will offend all the citizens equally. For, as Antonio Perez [2] excellently observes, an absolute dominion is to the prince very dangerous, to the subjects very hateful, and to the institutes of God and man alike opposed, as innumerable instances show.

15. Besides these we have, in the last chapter, laid other foundations, by which the king is greatly secured in his dominion, and the citizens in their hold of peace and liberty, which foundations we will reason out in their proper places. For I was anxious above everything to reason out all those, which refer to the great council and are of the greatest importance.

[2] Antonio Perez, a publicist, and professor of law in the University of Louvain in the first part of the seventeenth century.

Now I will continue with the others, in the same order in which I stated them.

16. It is undoubted, that citizens are more powerful, and, therefore, more independent, the larger and better fortified their towns are. For the safer the place is, in which they are, the better they can defend their liberty, and the less they need fear an enemy, whether without or within; and it is certain that the more powerful men are by their riches, the more they by nature study their own safety. But cities which need the help of another for their preservation are not on terms of equal right with that other, but are so far dependent on his right as they need his help. For we showed in the second chapter, that right is determined by power alone.

17. For the same reason, also, I mean that the citizens may continue independent, and defend their liberty, the militia ought to be composed of the citizens only, and none of them to be exempted. For an armed man is more independent than an unarmed (Sec. 12); and those citizens transfer absolutely their own right to another, and entrust it entirely to his good faith, who have given him their arms and the defences of their cities. Human avarice, by which most men are very much led, adds its weight to this view. For it cannot be, that a mercenary force be hired without great expense; and citizens can hardly endure the exactions required to maintain an idle soldiery. But that no man, who commands the whole or a large part of the militia, should, except under pressure of necessity, be chosen for the extreme term of a year, all are aware, who have read history, alike sacred and profane. For there is nothing that reason more clearly teaches. For surely the might of dominion is altogether entrusted to him, who is allowed enough time to gain military glory, and raise his fame above the king's, or to make the army faithful to himself by flattery, largesses, and the other arts, whereby generals are accustomed to procure the

enslavement of others, and the mastery for themselves. Lastly, I have added this point for the greater safety of the whole dominion, that these commanders of the militia are to be selected from the king's counsellors or ex-counsellors—that is, from men who have reached the age at which mankind generally prefer what is old and safe to what is new and dangerous.[3]

18. I said that the citizens were to be divided into clans,[4] and an equal number of counsellors chosen from each, in order that the larger towns might have, in proportion to the number of their citizens, a greater number of counsellors, and be able, as is equitable, to contribute more votes. For the power and, therefore, the right of a dominion is to be estimated by the number of its citizens; and I do not believe that any fitter means can be devised for maintaining this equality between citizens, who are all by nature so constituted, that everyone wishes to be attributed to his own stock, and be distinguished by race from the rest.

19. Furthermore, in the state of nature, there is nothing which any man can less claim for himself, and make his own, than the soil, and whatever so adheres to the soil, that he cannot hide it anywhere, nor carry it whither he pleases. The soil, therefore, and whatever adheres to it in the way we have mentioned, must be quite common property of the commonwealth —that is, of all those who, by their united force, can vindicate their claim to it, or of him to whom all have given authority to vindicate his claim. And therefore the soil, and all that adheres to it, ought to have a value with the citizens proportionate to the necessity there is, that they may be able to set their feet thereon, and defend their common right or liberty. But in the eighth section of this chapter we have shown the

[3] Chap. VI. Sec. 10.
[4] Chap. VI. Secs. 11, 15, 16.

advantages that the commonwealth must necessarily derive hence.

20. In order that the citizens may be as far as possible equal, which is of the first necessity in a commonwealth, none but the descendants of a king are to be thought noble. But if all the descendants of kings were allowed to marry wives, or beget children, they would grow, in process of time, to a very large number, and would be, not only burdensome, but also a cause of very great fear, to king and all. For men who have too much leisure generally meditate crime. And hence it is that kings are, on account of their nobles, very much induced to make war, because kings surrounded with nobles find more quiet and safety in war than in peace. But I pass by this as notorious enough, and also the points which I have mentioned in Secs. 15-27 of the last chapter. For the main points have been proved in this chapter, and the rest are self-evident.

21. That the judges ought to be too numerous for a large proportion of them to be accessible to the bribes of a private man, and that they should not vote openly, but secretly, and that they deserve payment for their time, is known to everyone.[5] But they everywhere have by custom a yearly salary; and so they make no great haste to determine suits, and there is often no end to trials. Next, where confiscations accrue to the king, there frequently in trials not truth nor right, but the greatness of a man's riches is regarded. Informers are ever at work, and everyone who has money is snatched as a prey, which evils, though grievous and intolerable, are excused by the necessity of warfare, and continue even in time of peace. But the avarice of judges that are appointed but for two or three years at most is moderated by fear of their successors, not to mention, again, that they can have no fixed property, but must lend their money at interest to their fellow-citizens.

[5] Chap. VI. Secs. 27, 28.

And so they are forced rather to consult their welfare than to plot against them, especially if the judges themselves, as we have said, are numerous.

22. But we have said, that no military pay is to be voted.[6] For the chief reward of military service is liberty. For in the state of nature everyone strives, for bare liberty's sake, to defend himself to the utmost of his power, and expects no other reward of warlike virtue but his own independence. But, in the civil state, all the citizens together are to be considered as a man in the state of nature; and, therefore, when all fight on behalf of that state, all are defending themselves, and engaged on their own business. But counsellors, judges, magistrates, and the like, are engaged more on others' business than on their own; and so it is but fair to pay them for their time. Besides, in war, there can be no greater or more honourable inducement to victory than the idea of liberty. But if, on the contrary, a certain portion of the citizens be designated as soldiers, on which account it will be necessary to award them a fixed pay, the king will, of necessity, distinguish them above the rest (as we showed, Sec. 12)—that is, will distinguish men who are acquainted only with the arts of war, and, in time of peace, from excess of leisure, become debauched, and, finally, from poverty, meditate nothing but rapine, civil discord, and wars. And so we can affirm, that a monarchy of this sort is, in fact, a state of war, and in it only the soldiery enjoy liberty, but the rest are slaves.

23. Our remarks about the admission of foreigners (Chap. VI. Sec. 32) I believe to be obvious. Besides, no one can doubt that the king's blood-relations should be at a distance from him, and occupied, not by warlike, but by peaceful business, whence they may get credit and the dominion quiet. Though even this has not seemed a sufficient precaution to the Turkish

6 Chap. VI. Sec. 31.

despots, who, therefore, make a point of slaughtering all their brothers. And no wonder: for the more absolutely the right of dominion has been conferred on one man, the more easily, as we showed by an instance (Sec. 14), it can be transferred from one to another. But that in such a monarchy, as we here suppose, in which, I mean, there is not one mercenary soldier, the plan we have mentioned provides sufficiently for the king's safety, is not to be doubted.

24. Nor can anyone hesitate about what we have said in the thirty-fourth and thirty-fifth sections of the last chapter. But that the king must not marry a foreigner [7] is easily proved. For not to mention that two commonwealths, although united by a treaty, are yet in a state of hostility (Chap. III. Sec. 14), it is very much to be avoided that war should be stirred up, on account of the king's domestic affairs, both because disputes and dissensions arise peculiarly from an alliance founded on marriage, and because questions between two commonwealths are mostly settled by war. Of this we read a fatal instance in Scripture. For after the death of Solomon, who had married the king of Egypt's daughter, his son Rehoboam waged a most disastrous war with Shishak, king of the Egyptians, who utterly subdued him. Moreover, the marriage of Lewis XIV., king of France with the daughter of Philip IV. was the seed of a fresh war.[8] And, besides these, very many instances may be read in history.

25. The form of the dominion ought to be kept one and the same, and, consequently, there should be but one king, and that of the same sex, and the dominion should be indivisible.[9] But as to my saying that the king's eldest son should succeed

---

[7] Chap. VI. Sec. 36.

[8] The war between France and Spain, terminated by the first peace of Aix-la-Chapelle, 1665.

[9] Chap. VI. Sec. 37.

his father by right, or (if there be no issue) the nearest to him in blood, it is clear as well from Chap. VI. Sec. 13, as because the election of the king made by the multitude should, if possible, last for ever. Otherwise it will necessarily happen, that the supreme authority of the dominion will frequently pass to the multitude, which is an extreme and, therefore, exceedingly dangerous change. But those who, from the fact that the king is master of the dominion, and holds it by absolute right, infer that he can hand it over to whom he pleases, and that, therefore, the king's son is by right heir to the dominion, are greatly mistaken. For the king's will has so long the force of law, as he holds the sword of the commonwealth; for the right of dominion is limited by power only. Therefore, a king may indeed abdicate, but cannot hand the dominion over to another, unless with the concurrence of the multitude or its stronger part. And that this may be more clearly understood, we must remark, that children are heirs to their parents, not by natural, but by civil law. For by the power of the commonwealth alone is anyone master of definite property. And, therefore, by the same power or right, whereby the will of any man concerning his property is held good, by the same also his will remains good after his own death, as long as the commonwealth endures. And this is the reason, why everyone in the civil state maintains after death the same right as he had in his lifetime, because, as we said, it is not by his own power, but by that of the commonwealth, which is everlasting, that he can decide anything about his property. But the king's case is quite different. For the king's will is the civil law itself, and the king the commonwealth itself. Therefore, by the death of the king, the commonwealth is in a manner dead, and the civil state naturally returns to the state of nature, and consequently the supreme authority to the multitude, which can, therefore, lawfully lay down new and abolish old laws. And so it appears that no man succeeds the king by right, but him whom the multitude wills to be successor, or in a theocracy, such as the commonwealth of the Hebrews once was, him whom God has chosen by a prophet. We might likewise infer this from the fact that the king's sword, or right, is in reality the will of the multitude itself, or its stronger part; or else from the fact, that men endowed with reason never so utterly abdicate their right, that they cease to be men, and are accounted as sheep. But to pursue this further is unnecessary.

26. But the right of religion, or of worshipping God, no man can transfer to another. However, we have treated of this point at length in the last chapters of our Theologico-Political Treatise,[10] which it is superfluous to repeat here. And herewith I claim to have reasoned out the foundations of the best monarchy, though briefly, yet with sufficient clearness. But their mutual interdependence, or, in other words, the proportions of my dominion, anyone will easily remark, who will be at the pains to observe them as a whole with some attention. It remains only to warn the reader, that I am here conceiving of that monarchy, which is instituted by a free multitude, for which alone these foundations can serve. For a multitude that has grown used to another form of dominion will not be able without great danger of overthrow to pluck up the accepted foundations of the whole dominion, and change its entire fabric.

27. And what we have written will, perhaps, be received with derision by those who limit to the populace only the vices which are inherent in all mortals; and use such phrases as, "the mob, if it is not frightened, inspires no little fear," and "the populace is either a humble slave, or a haughty master," and "it has no truth or judgment," etc. But all have one common nature. Only we are deceived by power and refinement.

10 'Above, pp. 63-73.

Whence it comes that when two do the same thing we say, "this man may do it with impunity, that man may not;" not because the deed, but because the doer is different. Haughtiness is a property of rulers. Men are haughty, but by reason of an appointment for a year; how much more than nobles, that have their honours eternal! But their arrogance is glossed over with importance, luxury, profusion, and a kind of harmony of vices, and a certain cultivated folly, and elegant villainy, so that vices, each of which looked at separately is foul and vile, because it is then most conspicuous, appear to the inexperienced and untaught honourable and becoming. "The mob, too, if it is not frightened, inspires no little fear;" yes, for liberty and slavery are not easily mingled. Lastly, as for the populace being devoid of truth and judgment, that is nothing wonderful, since the chief business of the dominion is transacted behind its back, and it can but make conjectures from the little, which cannot be hidden. For it is an uncommon virtue to suspend one's judgment. So it is supreme folly to wish to transact everything behind the backs of the citizens, and to expect that they will not judge ill of the same, and will not give everything an unfavourable interpretation. For if the populace could moderate itself, and suspend its judgment about things with which it is imperfectly acquainted, or judge rightly of things by the little it knows already, it would surely be more fit to govern, than to be governed. But, as we said, all have the same nature. All grow haughty with rule, and cause fear if they do not feel it, and everywhere truth is generally transgressed by enemies or guilty people; especially where one or a few have mastery, and have respect in trials not to justice or truth, but to amount of wealth.

28. Besides, paid soldiers, that are accustomed to military discipline, and can support cold and hunger, are likely to despise a crowd of citizens as very inferior for storming towns

or fighting pitched battles. But that my dominion is, therefore, more unhappy or less durable, no one of sound mind will
affirm. But, on the contrary, everyone that judges things fairly
will admit, that that dominion is the most durable of all, which
can content itself with preserving what it has got, without
coveting what belongs to others, and strives, therefore, most
eagerly by every means to avoid war and preserve peace.

29. But I admit that the counsels of such a dominion can
hardly be concealed. But everyone will also admit with me that
it is far better for the right counsels of a dominion to be
known to its enemies, than for the evil secrets of tyrants to
be concealed from the citizens. They who can treat secretly of
the affairs of a dominion have it absolutely under their authority, and, as they plot against the enemy in time of war, so do
they against the citizens in time of peace. Now that this
secrecy is often serviceable to a dominion, no one can deny; but
that without it the said dominion cannot subsist, no one will
ever prove. But, on the contrary, to entrust affairs of state absolutely to any man is quite incompatible with the maintenance
of liberty; and so it is folly to choose to avoid a small loss by
means of the greatest of evils. But the perpetual refrain of those
who lust after absolute dominion is, that it is to the essential
interest of the commonwealth that its business be secretly transacted, and other like pretences, which end in the more hateful
a slavery, the more they are clothed with a show of utility.

30. Lastly, although no dominion, as far as I know, has ever
been founded on all the conditions we have mentioned, yet
from experience itself we shall be able to prove that this form
of monarchy is the best, if we consider the causes of the preservation and overthrow of any dominion that is not barbarous.
But this I could not do without greatly wearying the reader.
However, I cannot pass over in silence one instance, that seems
worth remembering: I mean the dominion of the Arragonese,

who showed a singular loyalty towards their kings, and with equal constancy preserved unbroken the constitution of the kingdom. For as soon as they had cast off the slavish yoke of the Moors, they resolved to choose themselves a king, but on what conditions they could not quite make up their minds, and they therefore determined to consult the sovereign pontiff of Rome. He, who in this matter certainly bore himself as Christ's vicar, blamed them for so obstinately wishing to choose a king, unwarned by the example of the Hebrews. However, if they would not change their minds, then he advised them not to choose a king, without first instituting customs equitable and suitable to the national genius, and above all he would have them create some supreme council, to balance the king's power like the ephors of the Lacedæmonians, and to have absolute right to determine the disputes, which might arise between the king and the citizens. So then, following this advice, they established the laws, which seemed to them most equitable, of which the supreme interpreter, and therefore supreme judge, was to be, not the king, but the council, which they call the Seventeen, and whose president has the title of Justice.[11] This Justice then, and the Seventeen, who are chosen for life, not by vote but by lot, have the absolute right of revising and annulling all sentences passed upon any citizen by other courts, civil or ecclesiastical, or by the king himself, so that every citizen had the right to summon the king himself before this council. Moreover, they once had the right of electing and deposing the king. But after the lapse of many years the king, Don Pedro, who is called the Dagger, by canvassing, bribery, promises, and every sort of practice, at length procured the revocation of this

---

[11] See Hallam's "History of the Middle Ages," Chap. IV., for the constitutional history of Arragon. Hallam calls the Justiza the Justiciary, but the literal translation, Justice, seems warranted by our own English use of the word to designate certain judges. [Elwes's note.]

right. And as soon as he gained his point, he cut off, or, as I would sooner believe, wounded his hand before them all, saying, that not without the loss of royal blood could subjects be allowed to choose their king.[12] Yet he effected this change, but upon this condition, "That the subjects have had and shall have the right of taking arms against any violence whatever, whereby any may wish to enter upon the dominion to their hurt, nay, against the king himself, or the prince, his heir, if he thus encroach." By which condition they certainly rather rectified than abolished that right. For, as we have shown (Chap. IV. Secs. 5, 6), a king can be deprived of the power of ruling, not by the civil law, but by the law of war, in other words the subjects may resist his violence with violence. Besides this condition they stipulated others, which do not concern our present design. Having by these customs given themselves a constitution to the mind of all, they continued for an incredible length of time unharmed, the king's loyalty towards his subjects being as great as theirs towards him. But after that the kingdom fell by inheritance to Ferdinand of Castile, who first had the surname of Catholic; this liberty of the Arragonese began to displease the Castilians, who therefore ceased not to urge Ferdinand to abolish these rights. But he, not yet being accustomed to absolute dominion, dared make no such attempt, but replied thus to his counsellors: that (not to mention that he had received the kingdom of Arragon on those terms, which they knew, and had most solemnly sworn to observe the same, and that it was inhuman to break his word) he was of opinion, that his kingdom would be stable, as long as its safety was as much to the subjects' as to the king's interest, so that neither

[12] Hallam says, that the king merely cut the obnoxious Privilege of Union, which he describes rather differently, through with his sword. The Privilege of Union was so utterly "eradicated from the records of the kingdom, that its precise words have never been recovered." [Elwes's note.]

the king should outweigh the subjects, nor yet the subjects the king; for that if either party were too powerful, the weaker would not only try to recover its former equality, but in vexation at its injury to retaliate upon the other, whence would follow the ruin of either or both. Which very wise language I could not enough wonder at, had it proceeded from a king accustomed to command not freemen but slaves. Accordingly the Arragonese retained their liberties after the time of Ferdinand, though no longer by right but by the favour of their too powerful kings, until the reign of Philip II., who oppressed them with better luck, but no less cruelty, than he did the United Provinces. And although Philip III. is supposed to have restored everything to its former position, yet the Arragonese, partly from eagerness to flatter the powerful (for it is folly to kick against the pricks), partly from terror, have kept nothing but the specious names and empty forms of liberty.

31. We conclude, therefore, that the multitude may preserve under a king an ample enough liberty; if it contrive that the king's power be determined by the sole power, and preserved by the defence of the multitude itself. And this was the single rule which I followed in laying the foundations of monarchy.

Chapter VIII

Of Aristocracy

SO far of monarchy. But now we will say, on what plan an aristocracy is to be framed, so that it may be lasting. We have defined an aristocratic dominion as that, which is held not by one man, but by certain persons chosen out of the multitude, whom we shall henceforth call patricians. I say expressly, "that which is held by certain persons chosen." For the chief difference between this and a democracy is, that the right of governing depends in an aristocracy on election only, but in a democracy for the most part on some right either congenital or acquired by fortune (as we shall explain in its place); and therefore, although in any dominion the entire multitude be received into the number of the patricians, provided that right of theirs is not inherited, and does not descend by some law to others, the dominion will for all that be quite an aristocracy, because none are received into the number of the patricians save by express election. But if these chosen persons were but two, each of them will try to be more powerful than the other, and from the too great power of each, the dominion will easily be split into two factions; and in like manner into three, four, or five factions, if three, four, or five persons were put into possession of it. But the factions will be the weaker, the more there are to whom the dominion was delegated. And hence it follows, that to secure the stability of an aristocracy, it is necessary to consider the proportionate size of the actual dominion, in order to determine the minimum number of patricians.

2. Let it be supposed, then, that for a dominion of moderate

size it suffices to be allowed a hundred of the best men, and that upon them has been conferred the supreme authority of the dominion, and that they have consequently the right to elect their patrician colleagues, when any of the number die. These men will certainly endeavour to secure their succession to their children or next in blood. And thus the supreme authority of the dominion will always be with those, whom fortune has made children or kinsmen to patricians. And, as out of a hundred men who rise to office by fortune, hardly three are found that excel in knowledge and counsel, it will thus come to pass, that the authority of the dominion will rest, not with a hundred, but only with two or three who excel by vigour of mind, and who will easily draw to themselves everything, and each of them, as is the wont of human greed, will be able to prepare the way to a monarchy. And so, if we make a right calculation, it is necessary, that the supreme authority of a dominion, whose size requires at least a hundred first-rate men, should be conferred on not less than five thousand. For by this proportion it will never fail, but a hundred shall be found excelling in mental vigour, that is, on the hypothesis that, out of fifty that seek and obtain office, one will always be found not less than first-rate, besides others that imitate the virtues of the first-rate, and are therefore worthy to rule.

3. The patricians are most commonly citizens of one city, which is the head of the whole dominion, so that the commonwealth or republic has its name from it, as once that of Rome, and now those of Venice, Genoa, etc. But the republic of the Dutch has its name from an entire province, whence it arises, that the subjects of this dominion enjoy a greater liberty. Now, before we can determine the foundations on which this aristocratic dominion ought to rest, we must observe a very great difference, which exists between the dominion which is conferred on one man and that which is conferred on a sufficiently

large council. For, in the first place, the power of one man is (as we said, Chap. VI. Sec. 5) very inadequate to support the entire dominion; but this no one, without manifest absurdity, can affirm of a sufficiently large council. For, in declaring the council to be sufficiently large, one at the same time denies, that it is inadequate to support the dominion. A king, therefore, is altogether in need of counsellors, but a council like this is not so in the least. In the second place, kings are mortal, but councils are everlasting. And so the power of the dominion which has once been transferred to a large enough council never reverts to the multitude. But this is otherwise in a monarchy, as we showed (Chap. VII. Sec. 25). Thirdly, a king's dominion is often on sufferance, whether from his minority, sickness, or old age, or from other causes; but the power of a council of this kind, on the contrary, remains always one and the same. In the fourth place, one man's will is very fluctuating and inconstant; and, therefore, in a monarchy, all law is, indeed, the explicit will of the king (as we said, Chap. VII. Sec. 1), but not every will of the king ought to be law; but this cannot be said of the will of a sufficiently numerous council. For since the council itself, as we have just shown, needs no counsellors, its every explicit will ought to be law. And hence we conclude, that the dominion conferred upon a large enough council is absolute, or approaches nearest to the absolute. For if there be any absolute dominion, it is, in fact, that which is held by an entire multitude.

4. Yet in so far as this aristocratic dominion never (as has just been shown) reverts to the multitude, and there is under it no consultation with the multitude, but, without qualification, every will of the council is law, it must be considered as quite absolute, and therefore its foundations ought to rest only on the will and judgment of the said council, and not on the watchfulness of the multitude, since the latter is excluded from

giving its advice or its vote. The reason, then, why in practice aristocracy is not absolute, is that the multitude is a cause of fear to the rulers, and therefore succeeds in retaining for itself some liberty, which it asserts and holds as its own, if not by an express law, yet on a tacit understanding.

5. And thus it is manifest that this kind of dominion will be in the best possible condition, if its institutions are such that it most nearly approaches the absolute—that is, that the multitude is as little as possible a cause of fear, and retains no liberty, but such as must necessarily be assigned it by the law of the dominion itself, and is therefore not so much a right of the multitude as of the whole dominion, asserted and maintained by the aristocrats only as their own. For thus practice agrees best with theory, as appears from the last section, and is also self-evident. For we cannot doubt that the dominion rests the less with the patricians, the more rights the commons assert for themselves, such as those which the corporations of artisans in Lower Germany, commonly called Guilds, generally possess.

6. But the commons need not apprehend any danger of a hateful slavery from this form of dominion, merely because it is conferred on the council absolutely. For the will of so large a council cannot be so much determined by lust as by reason; because men are drawn asunder by an evil passion, and cannot be guided, as it were, by one mind, except so far as they desire things honourable, or that have at least an honourable appearance.

7. In determining, then, the foundations of an aristocracy, it is above all to be observed, that they should rest on the sole will and power of the supreme council, so that it may be as independent as possible, and be in no danger from the multitude. In order to determine these foundations, which are to rest, I say, upon the sole will and power of the council, let us see what foundations of peace are peculiar to monarchy, and

unsuited to this form of dominion. For if we substitute for these equivalent foundations fit for an aristocracy, and leave the rest, as they are already laid, we shall have removed without doubt every cause of seditions; or, at least, this kind of dominion will be no less safe than the monarchical, but, on the contrary, so much the more so, and of so much better a condition, as, without danger to peace and liberty, it approaches nearer than monarchy to the absolute (Secs. 3, 6). For the greater the right of the supreme authority, the more the form of dominion agrees with the dictate of reason (Chap. III. Sec. 5), and, therefore, the fitter it is to maintain peace and liberty. Let us run through, therefore, the points we stated in our sixth chapter, beginning with the ninth section, that we may reject what is unfit for this kind of dominion, and see what agrees with it.

8. That it is necessary, in the first place, to found and fortify one or more cities, no one can doubt. But that city is above all to be fortified, which is the head of the whole dominion, and also those that are on its frontiers. For that which is the head of the whole dominion, and has the supreme right, ought to be more powerful than the rest. But under this kind of dominion it is quite unnecessary to divide all the inhabitants into clans.

9. As for the military, since under this dominion equality is not to be looked for among all, but between the patricians only, and, in particular, the power of the patricians is greater than that of the commons, it is certain that it makes no difference to the laws or fundamental principles of this dominion, that the military be formed of others besides subjects.[1] But it *is* of the first importance that no one be admitted into the number of the patricians, that has not a proper knowledge of the art of war. But for the subjects to be excluded, as some would have it, from military service, is surely folly. For besides that

[1] *Cf.* Chap. VI. Sec. 10.

the military pay given to subjects remains within the realm, whereas, on the contrary, what is paid to a foreign soldiery is altogether lost, the greatest strength of the dominion is also thereby weakened. For it is certain that those fight with peculiar valour who fight for altar and hearth. Whence, also, it is manifest that those are no less wrong, who lay down that military commanders, tribunes, centurions, etc., should be chosen from among the patricians only. For with what courage will those soldiers fight who are deprived of all hope of gaining glory and advancement? But, on the other hand, to establish a law forbidding the patricians to hire foreign soldiers when circumstances require it, whether to defend themselves, and suppress seditions, or for any other reason, besides being inconsiderate, would also be repugnant to the supreme right of the patricians, concerning which see Secs. 3, 4, 5 of this chapter. But the general of a single army, or of the entire military, is to be chosen but in time of war, and among the patricians only, and is to hold the command for a year at most, without power of being continued therein, or afterwards reappointed. For this law, necessary as it is under a monarchy, is so above all under this kind of dominion. For although it is much easier, as we have said above, to transfer the dominion from one man to another than from a free council to one man; yet it does often happen, that particians are subdued by their own generals, and that to the much greater harm of the commonwealth. For when a monarch is removed, it is but a change of tyrant, not of the form of dominion; but, under an aristocracy, this cannot happen, without an upsetting of the form of dominion, and a slaughter of the greatest men. Of which thing Rome has offered the most mournful examples. But our reason for saying that, under a monarchy, the militia should serve without pay, is here inapplicable. For since the subjects are excluded from giving their advice or votes, they are to be reckoned as foreigners, and are, therefore, to be hired for service on no worse terms than foreigners. And there is in this case no danger of their being distinguished above the rest by the patricians: nay, further, to avoid the partial judgment which everyone is apt to form of his own exploits, it is wiser for the patricians to assign a fixed payment to the soldiers for their service.

10. Furthermore, for this same reason, that all but the patricians are foreigners, it cannot be without danger to the whole dominion, that the lands and houses and the whole soil should remain public property, and be let to the inhabitants at a yearly rent. For the subjects having no part in the dominion would easily, in bad times, all forsake their cities, if they could carry where they pleased what goods they possess. And, therefore, lands and farms are not to be let, but sold to the subjects, yet on condition that they pay every year an aliquot part of the year's produce, etc., as is done in Holland.

11. These points considered, I proceed to the foundations on which the supreme council should rest and be established. We have shown (Sec. 2) that, in a moderate-sized dominion, this council ought to have about five thousand members. And so we must look for means of preventing the dominion from gradually getting into fewer hands, and of insuring, on the contrary, that the number of members be increased in proportion to the growth of the dominion itself; and, next, that between the patricians, equality be as far as possible maintained; and, further, that there may be speed and expedition in their counsels, and that they tend to the general good; and, lastly, that the power of the patricians or council exceed the power of the multitude, yet so that the multitude suffer no harm thereby.

12. But jealousy causes a great difficulty in maintaining our first point. For men are, as we have said, by nature enemies, so that however they be associated, and bound together by

laws, they still retain their nature. And hence I think it is, that democracies change into aristocracies, and these at length into monarchies. For I am fully persuaded that most aristocracies were formerly democracies. For when a given multitude, in search of fresh territories, has found and cultivated them, it retains, as a whole, its equal right of dominion, because no man gives dominion to another spontaneously. But although every one of them thinks it fair, that he should have the same right against another that that other has against him, he yet thinks it unfair, that the foreigners that join them should have equal right in the dominion with themselves, who sought it by their own toil, and won it at the price of their own blood. And this not even the foreigners themselves deny, for, of course, they migrate thither, not to hold dominion, but for the benefit of their own private business, and are quite satisfied if they are but allowed the liberty of transacting that business in safety. But meanwhile the multitude is augmented by the influx of foreigners, who gradually acquire the national manners, until at last they are distinguished by no other difference than that of incapacity to get office; and while their number daily increases, that of the citizens, on the contrary, is by many causes diminished. For families often die out, and some persons are disqualified for their crimes, and a great many are driven by domestic poverty to neglect affairs of state, and meanwhile the more powerful aim at nothing else, but to govern alone; and thus the dominion is gradually limited to a few, and at length by faction to one. And here we might add other causes that destroy dominions of this sort; but as they are well known, I pass them by, and proceed now to state the laws by which this dominion, of which we are treating, ought to be maintained.

13. The primary law of this dominion ought to be that which determines the proportionate numbers of patricians and multi-

tude. For a proportion (Sec. 1) ought to be maintained between the multitude and the patricians, so that with the increase of the former the number of the latter should be raised. And this proportion (in accordance with our remarks in the second section) ought to be about fifty to one, that is, the inequality between the members of each should never be greater. For (Sec. 1) without destroying the form of dominion, the number of patricians may be greater than the number of the multitude. But there is no danger except in the smallness of their number. But how it is to be provided that this law be kept unbroken, I will presently show in its own place.

14. Patricians, in some places, are chosen only out of particular families. But it is ruinous to lay this down expressly by law. For not to mention that families often die out, and that the other families can never be excluded without disgrace, it is also repugnant to the form of this dominion, that the dignity of patrician should be hereditary (Sec. 1). But on this system a dominion seems rather a democracy, such as we have described in Sec. 12, that is in the hands of very few citizens. But, on the other hand, to provide against the patricians choosing their own sons and kinsmen, and thereby against the right of dominion remaining in particular families, is impossible, and indeed absurd, as I shall show (Sec. 39). But provided that they hold that right by no express law, and that the rest (I mean, such as are born within the dominion, and use the vulgar tongue, and have not a foreign wife, and are not infamous, nor servants, nor earning their living by any servile trade, among which are to be reckoned those of a wine-merchant, or brewer) are not excluded, the form of the dominion will, notwithstanding, be retained, and it will be possible to maintain the proportion between the patricians and the multitude.

15. But if it be further by law appointed that no young men

be chosen, it will never happen that a few families hold the right of government in their hands. And, therefore, be it by law appointed, that no man that has not reached his thirtieth year be put on the list of candidates.

16. Thirdly, it is next to be ordained, that all the patricians must be assembled at certain fixed times in a particular part of the city, and that whoever does not attend the council, unless he be hindered by illness or some public business, shall be fined some considerable amount. For, were it otherwise, most of them would neglect the public, for the sake of their own private affairs.

17. Let this council's functions be to pass and repeal laws, and to choose their patrician colleagues, and all the ministers of the dominion. For he, that has supreme right, as we have decided that this council has, cannot give to anyone authority to pass and repeal laws, without at the same time abdicating his own right, and transferring it to him, to whom he gives that power. For he, that has but for one day only authority to pass and repeal laws, is able to change the entire form of the dominion. But one can, without forfeiting one's supreme right, temporarily entrust to others the daily business of dominion to be administered according to the established laws. Furthermore, if the ministers of dominion were chosen by any other but this council, then its members would be more properly called wards than patricians.

18. Hence some are accustomed to create for the council a ruler or prince, either for life, as the Venetians, or for a time, as the Genoese; but yet with such great precautions, as make it clear enough, that it is not done without great risk. And assuredly we cannot doubt but that the dominion thereby approaches the monarchical form, and as far as we can conjecture from their histories, it was done for no other reason, than that before the institution of these councils they had lived under a

ruler, or doge, as under a king. And so the creation of a ruler is a necessary requisite indeed for the particular nation, but not for the aristocratic dominion considered in itself.

19. But, inasmuch as the supreme authority of this dominion rests with this council as a whole, not with every individual member of it (for otherwise it would be but the gathering of an undisciplined mob), it is, therefore, necessary that all the patricians be so bound by the laws as to form, as it were, one body governed by one mind. But the laws by themselves alone are weak and easily broken, when their vindicators are the very persons who are able to transgress them, and the only ones who are to take warning by the punishment, and must punish their colleagues in order by fear of the same punishment to restrain their own desire: for all this involves a great absurdity. And, therefore, means must be sought to preserve order in this supreme council and keep unbroken the constitution of the dominion, so that yet the greatest possible equality may exist between patricians.

20. But since, from a single ruler or prince, able also to vote in the debates, there must necessarily arise a great inequality, especially on account of the power, which must of necessity be granted him, in order to enable him to discharge his duty in safety; therefore, if we consider the whole matter aright, nothing can be devised more useful to the general welfare than the institution of another council of certain patricians subordinate to the supreme council, whose only duty should be to see that the constitution, as far as it concerns the councils and ministers of the dominion, be kept unbroken, and who should, therefore, have authority to summon to judgment and, in conformity with established law, to condemn any delinquent who, as a minister of the dominion, has transgressed the laws concerning his office. And these patricians we shall hereafter call syndics.

21. And they are to be chosen for life. For, were they to be chosen for a time, so that they should afterwards be eligible for other offices in the dominion, we should fall into the very absurdity which we have just pointed out in the nineteenth section. But lest they should become quite haughty by very long rule, none are to be elected to this office, but those who have reached their sixtieth year or more, and have discharged the duties of senator, of which below.

22. Of these, too, we shall easily determine the number, if we consider that these syndics stand to the patricians in the same relation as the whole body of patricians together does to the multitude, which they cannot govern, if they are fewer than a proper number. And, therefore, the number of the syndics should be to that of patricians as their number is to that of the multitude, that is (Sec. 13), as one to fifty.

23. Moreover, that this council may discharge its functions in security, some portion of the soldiery must be assigned to it, and be subject to its orders.

24. The syndics and other ministers of state are to have no salary, but such emoluments, that they cannot maladminster affairs of state without great loss to themselves. For we cannot doubt that it is fair, that the ministers of this kind of dominion should be awarded a recompense for their time, since the commons are the majority in this dominion, and the patricians look after their safety, while they themselves have no trouble with affairs of state, but only with their own private ones. But since, on the other hand, no man (Chap. VII. Sec. 4) defends another's cause, save in so far as he thereby hopes to establish his own interest, things must, of necessity, be so ordered that the ministers, who have charge of affairs of state, should most pursue their own interest, when they are most watchful for the general good.

25. To the syndics then, whose duty, as we said, it is to see

that the constitution is kept unbroken, the following emoluments are to be awarded: namely, that every householder that inhabits any place in the dominion, be bound to pay every year a coin of small value, say a quarter of an ounce of silver, to the syndics, that thus they may know the number of inhabitants, and so observe what proportion of them the patricians constitute; and next that every new patrician on his election must pay the syndics some large sum, for instance, twenty or twenty-five pounds of silver. Moreover, that money, in which the absent patricians (I mean those who have failed to attend the meeting of the council) are condemned, is also to be awarded to the syndics; and a part, too, of the goods of defaulting ministers, who are bound to abide their judgment, and who are fined a certain sum of money, or have their goods confiscated, should be devoted to them, not to all indeed, but to those only who sit daily, and whose duty it is to summon the council of syndics, concerning whom see Sec. 28. But, in order that the council of syndics may always be maintained at its full number, before all other business in the supreme council, when it is assembled at the usual time, inquiry is to be made about this. Which, if the syndics neglect, let it then devolve upon the president of the senate (concerning which we shall soon have occasion to speak), to admonish the supreme council on this head, to demand of the president of the syndics the reason of his silence, and to inquire what is the supreme council's opinion in the matter. But if the president of the senate is likewise silent, let the case be taken up by the president of the supreme court of justice, or if he too is silent by some other patrician, and let him demand an explanation of their silence from the presidents of the senate and the court of justice, as well as from the president of the syndics. Lastly, that that law, whereby young men are excluded, may likewise be strictly observed, it is to be appointed that all who have reached the thirtieth year of their age, and who are not by express law excluded, are to have their names inscribed on a list, in presence of the syndics, and to receive from them, at a fixed price, some sign of the honour conferred on them, namely, that they may be allowed to wear a particular ornament only permitted to them, to distinguish them and make them to be had in honour by the rest; and, at the same time, be it ordained, that in elections none may nominate as patrician anyone whose name is not inscribed on the general list, and that under a heavy penalty. And, further, let no one be allowed to refuse the burden of a duty or office, which he is chosen to bear. Lastly, that all the absolutely fundamental laws of the dominion may be everlasting, it must be ordained that if anyone in the supreme council raise a question about any fundamental law, as of prolonging the command of any general of an army, or of diminishing the number of patricians, or the like, he is guilty of treason, and not only is he to be condemned to death, and his goods confiscated, but some sign of his punishment is to remain visible in public for an eternal memorial of the event. But for the confirming of the other general rights of the dominion, it is enough, if it be only ordained, that no law can be repealed nor new law passed, unless first the college of syndics, and then three-fourths or four-fifths of the supreme council agree thereto.

26. Let the right also of summoning the supreme council and proposing the matters to be decided in it, rest with the syndics, and let them likewise be given the first place in the council, but without the right to vote. But before they take their seats, they must swear by the safety of that supreme council and by the public liberty, that they will strive with the utmost zeal to preserve unbroken the ancient laws, and to consult the general good. After which let them through their secretary open in order the subjects of discussion.

27. But that all the patricians may have equal authority in making decrees and electing the ministers of the dominion, and that speed and expedition in all matters may be possible, the order observed by the Venetians is altogether to be approved, for they appoint by lot a certain number of the council to name the ministers, and when these have named in order the candidates for office, every patrician signifies by ballot his opinion, approving or rejecting the candidate in question, so that it is not afterwards known, who voted in this or that sense. Whereby it is contrived, not only that the authority of all the patricians in the decision is equal, and that business is quickly despatched, but also, that everyone has absolute liberty (which is of the first necessity in councils) to give his opinion without danger of unpopularity.

28. But in the councils of syndics and the other councils, the same order is to be observed, that voting is to be by ballot. But the right of convoking the council of syndics and of proposing the matters to be decided in the same ought to belong to their president, who is to sit every day with ten or more other syndics, to hear the complaints and secret accusations of the commons against the ministers, and to look after the accusers, if circumstances require, and to summon the supreme council even before the appointed time, if any of them judge that there is danger in the delay. Now this president and those who meet with him every day are to be appointed by the supreme council and out of the number of syndics, not indeed for life, but for six months, and they must not have their term renewed but after the lapse of three or four years. And these, as we said above, are to be awarded the goods that are confiscated and the pecuniary fines, or some part of them. The remaining points which concern the syndics we will mention in their proper places.

29. The second council, which is subordinate to the supreme

one, we will call the senate, and let its duty be to transact public business, for instance, to publish the laws of the dominion, to order the fortifications of the cities according to law, to confer military commissions, to impose taxes on the subjects and apply the same, to answer foreign embassies, and decide where embassies are to be sent. But let the actual appointment of ambassadors be the duty of the supreme council. For it is of the greatest consequence to see that no patrician be called to any office in the dominion but by the supreme council itself, lest the patricians themselves should try to curry favour with the senate. Secondly, all matters are to be referred to the supreme council, which in any way alter the existing state of things, as the deciding on peace and war. Wherefore, that the senate's decrees concerning peace and war may be valid, they must be confirmed by the supreme council. And therefore I should say, that it belonged to the supreme council only, not to the senate, to impose new taxes.

30. In determining the number of senators these points are to be taken into consideration: first, that all the patricians should have an equal hope of gaining senatorial rank; secondly, that notwithstanding the same senators, whose time (for which they were elected) is elapsed, may be continued after a short interval, that so the dominion may always be governed by skilled and experienced men; and lastly, that among the senators many may be found illustrious for wisdom and virtue. But to secure all these conditions, there can be no other means devised, than that it should be by law appointed, that no one who has not reached his fiftieth year, be received into the number of senators, and that four hundred, that is about a twelfth part of the patricians, be appointed for a year, and that two years after that year has elapsed, the same be capable of re-appointment. For in this manner about a twelfth part of the patricians will be constantly engaged in the duty of senator,

with only short intervening periods; and this number surely, together with that made up by the syndics, will be little less than the number of patricians that have attained their fiftieth year. And so all the patricians will always have a great hope of gaining the rank of senator or syndic, and yet notwithstanding, the same patricians, at only short intervals, will always hold senatorial rank, and (according to what we said, Sec. 2) there will never be wanting in the senate distinguished men, excelling in counsel and skill. And because this law cannot be broken without exciting great jealousy on the part of many patricians, it needs no other safeguard for its constant validity, than that every patrician who has reached the age we mentioned, should offer the proof thereof to the syndics, who shall put his name on the list of candidates for the senatorial duties, and read the name before the supreme council, so that he may occupy, with the rest of the same rank, a place set apart in this supreme council for his fellows, next to the place of the senators.

31. The emoluments of the senators should be of such a kind, that their profit is greater from peace than from war. And therefore let there be awarded to them a hundredth or a fiftieth part of the merchandise exported abroad from the dominion, or imported into it from abroad. For we cannot doubt, that by this means they will, as far as they can, preserve peace, and never desire to protract war. And from this duty not even the senators themselves, if any of them are merchants, ought to be exempt; for such an immunity cannot be granted without great risk to trade, as I think no one is ignorant. Nay, on the contrary, it must be by law ordained, that no senator or ex-senator may fill any military post; and further, that no one may be declared general or prætor, which officers we said (Sec. 9) were to be only appointed in time of war, whose father or grandfather is a senator, or has held the dignity of

senator within two years. Which laws we cannot doubt, that
the patricians outside the senate will defend with all their
might: and so it will be the case, that the senators will always
have more profit from peace than from war, and will, therefore, never advise war, except the utmost need of the dominion
compels them. But it may be objected to us, that on this system, if, that is, syndics and senators are to be allowed so great
profits, an aristocracy will be as burdensome to the subjects
as any monarchy. But not to mention that royal courts require
larger expenditure, and are yet not provided in order to secure
peace, and that peace can never be bought too dear; it is to be
added, first, that all that under a monarchy is conferred on one
or a few, is here conferred upon very many. Next kings and
their ministers do not bear the burden of the dominion with
the subjects, but under this form of dominion it is just the
reverse; for the patricians, who are always chosen from the
rich, bear the largest share of the weight of the commonwealth.
Lastly, the burdens of a monarchy spring not so much from
its king's expenditure, as from its secret policy. For those burdens of a dominion, that are imposed on the citizens in order
to secure peace and liberty, great though they be, are yet supported and lightened by the usefulness of peace. What nation
ever had to pay so many and so heavy taxes as the Dutch?
Yet it not only has not been exhausted, but, on the contrary,
has been so mighty by its wealth, that all envied its good
fortune. If therefore the burdens of a monarchy were imposed
for the sake of peace, they would not oppress the citizens; but,
as I have said, it is from the secret policy of that sort of
dominion, that the subjects faint under their lord; that is,
because the virtue of kings counts for more in time of war
than in time of peace, and because they, who would reign by
themselves, ought above all to try and have their subjects poor;
not to mention other things, which that most prudent Dutch-

man V. H.[2] formerly remarked, because they do not concern my design, which is only to describe the best state of every kind of dominion.

32. Of the syndics chosen by the supreme council, some should sit in the senate, but without the right of voting, so that they may see whether the laws concerning that assembly be duly observed, and may have the supreme council convoked, when anything is to be referred to it from the senate. For the supreme right of convoking this council, and proposing to it subjects of discussion, is, as we have already said, with the syndics. But before the votes of the contemporaries of the senators be taken, the president of the senate for the time being shall explain the state of affairs, and what the senator's own opinion is on the matter in question, and why; after which the votes shall be collected in the accustomed order.

33. The entire senate ought not to meet every day, but, like all great councils, at a certain fixed time. But as in the mean time the business of the dominion must be executed, it is, therefore, necessary that some part of the senators be chosen, who, on the dismissal of the senate, shall supply its place, and whose duty it shall be to summon the senate itself, when need is; to execute its orders about affairs of state; to read letters written to the senate and supreme council; and, lastly, to consult about the matters to be proposed in the senate. But that all these points, and the order of this assembly, as a whole, may be more easily conceived, I will describe the whole matter more precisely.

34. The senators who, as we have said already, are to be chosen for a year, are to be divided into four or six series, of

2 "This V. H. is Pieter de la Court (1618-85), an eminent publicist, who wrote under the initials D. C. (De la Court), V. H. (Van den Hove, the Dutch equivalent). He was a friend of John de Witt, and opposed to the party of the Statholders."—Pollock's *Life and Philosophy of Spinoza,* towards end of Chap. X.

which let the first have the first seat in the senate for the first
three or two months in the year; and at the expiration of this
time, let the second series take the place of the first, and so on,
observing their turns, so that that series which was first in the
first months may be last in the second period. Furthermore,
there are to be appointed as many presidents as there are series,
and the same number of vice-presidents to fill their places when
required—that is, two are to be chosen out of every series, one
to be its president, the other its vice-president. And let the
president of the first series preside in the senate also, for the
first months; or, in his absence, let his vice-president fill his
place; and so on with the rest, observing the same order as
above. Next, out of the first series, some are to be chosen by
vote or lot to fill the place of the senate, when it is dismissed,
in conjunction with the president and vice-president of the
same series; and that, for the same space of time, as the said
series occupies the first place in the senate; and thus, when that
time is past, as many are again to be chosen out of the second
series, by vote or lot, to fill, in conjunction with their president
and vice-president, the place of the first series, and supply the
lack of a senate; and so on with the rest. And there is no need
that the election of these men—I mean those that I have said
are to be chosen for periods of three or two months, by vote
or lot—should be made by the supreme council. For the reason
which we gave in the twenty-ninth section is not here applicable, much less the reason stated in the seventeenth. It suffices,
then, that they be elected by the senate and the syndics present
at its meeting.

35. But of these persons we cannot so precisely ascertain the
number. However, this is certain, that they must be too numerous to be easily susceptible of corruption. For though they can
by themselves determine nothing concerning affairs of state,
yet they can delay the senate, or, what would be worst of all,

delude it by putting forward matters of no importance, and keeping back those that are of greater—not to mention that, if they were too few, the absence of one or two might delay public business. But as, on the contrary, these consuls are for that very reason appointed, because great councils cannot devote themselves every day to public business, a remedy must be looked for necessarily here, and their inadequacy of number be made up for by the shortness of their term of office. And thus, if only thirteen or so be chosen for two or three months, they will be too many to be corrupted in this short period. And for this cause, also, did I recommend that their successors should by no means be appointed, except at the very time when they do succeed, and the others go away.

36. We have said, that it is also their duty, when any, though few, of them think it needful, to convoke the senate, to put before it the matters to be decided, to dismiss it, and to execute its orders about public business. But I will now briefly state the order in which this ought to be done, so that business may not be long protracted by useless questions. Let, then, the consuls consult about the matter to be proposed in the senate, and what is required to be done; and, if they are all of one mind about it, then let them convoke the senate, and, having duly explained the question, let them set forth what their opinion is, and, without waiting for another's opinion, collect the votes in their order. But if the consuls support more than one opinion, then, in the senate, that opinion is first to be stated on the question proposed, which was supported by the larger number of consuls. And if the same is not approved by the majority of senate and consuls, but the waverers and opponents together are in a majority, which is to be determined by ballot, as we have already mentioned, then let them set forth the second opinion, which had fewer votes than the former among the consuls, and so on with the rest. But if none be approved by a

majority of the whole senate, the senate is to be adjourned to the next day, or for a short time, that the consuls meanwhile may see, if they can find other means, that may give more satisfaction. But if they do not succeed in finding other means, or if the majority of the senate refuses to approve such as they have found, then the opinion of every senator is to be heard; and if the majority of the senate also refuses to support any of these, then the votes are to be taken again on every opinion, and not only the affirmative votes, as hitherto, but the doubtful and negative are to be counted. And if the affirmative prove more numerous than the doubtful or negative, then that opinion is to hold good; but, on the contrary, to be lost, if the negative prove more numerous than the doubtful or affirmative. But if on every opinion there is a greater number of doubters than of voters for and against, then let the council of syndics join the senate, and vote with the senators, with only affirmative and negative votes, omitting those that signify a hesitating mind. And the same order is to be observed about matters referred by the senate to the supreme council. So much for the senate.

37. As for the court of justice or bench, it cannot rest upon the same foundations as that which exists under a monarch, as we described it in Chap. VI. Secs. 26, and following. For (Sec. 14) it agrees not with the foundations of our present dominion, that any account be made of families or clans. And there must be a further difference, because judges chosen from the patricians only might indeed be restrained by the fear of their patrician successors, from pronouncing any unjust judgment against any of the patricians, and, perhaps, would hardly have the courage to punish them after their deserts; but they would, on the other hand, dare everything against the commons, and daily carry off the rich among them for a prey. I know that the plan of the Genoese is therefore approved by many, for they

choose their judges not among the patricians, but among foreigners. But this seems to me, considering the matter in the abstract, absurdly ordained, that foreigners and not patricians should be called in to interpret the laws. For what are judges but interpreters of the laws? And I am therefore persuaded that herein also the Genoese have had regard rather to the genius of their own race, than to the very nature of this kind of dominion. We must, therefore, by considering the matter in the abstract, devise the means which best agree with the form of this government.

38. But as far as regards the number of the judges, the theory of this constitution requires no peculiar number; but as under monarchical dominion, so under this, it suffices that they be too numerous to be corrupted by a private man. For their duty is but to provide against one private person doing wrong to another, and therefore to decide disputes between private persons, as well patricians as commons, and to exact penalties from delinquents, and even from patricians, syndics, and senators, as far as they have offended against the laws, whereby all are bound. But disputes that may arise between cities that are subject to the dominion, are to be decided in the supreme council.

39. Furthermore the principle regulating the time, for which the judges should be appointed, is the same in both dominions, and also the principle of a certain part of them retiring every year; and, lastly, although it is not necessary for every one of them to be of a different family, yet it is necessary that two related by blood should not sit on the same bench together. And this last point is to be observed also in the other councils, except the supreme one, in which it is enough, if it be only provided by law that in elections no man may nominate a relation, nor vote upon his nomination by another, and also that two relations may not draw lots from the urn for the

nomination of any minister of the dominion. This, I say, is sufficient in a council that is composed of so large a number of men, and has no special profits assigned to it. And so utterly unharmed will the dominion be in this quarter, that it is absurd to pass a law excluding from the supreme council the relations of all the patricians, as we said in the fourteenth section. But that it is absurd is manifest. For that law could not be instituted by the patricians themselves, without their thereby all absolutely abdicating their own right, and therefore not the patricians themselves but the commons would defend this law, which is directly contrary to what we proved in Secs. 5 and 6. But that law of the dominion, whereby it is ordained that the same uniform proportion be maintained between the numbers of the patricians and the multitude, chiefly contemplates this end of preserving the patricians' right and power, that is, provides against their becoming too few to be able to govern the multitude.

40. But the judges are to be chosen by the supreme council out of the patricians only, that is (Sec. 17) out of the actual authors of the laws, and the judgments they pass, as well in civil as criminal cases, shall be valid, if they were pronounced in due course of justice and without partiality; into which matter the syndics shall be by law authorized to inquire, and to judge and determine thereof.

41. The judges' emoluments ought to be the same, as we mentioned in the twenty-ninth section of the sixth chapter; namely, that they receive from the losing party upon every judgment which they pass in civil cases, an aliquot part of the whole sum at stake. But as to their sentences in criminal cases, let there be here this difference only, that the goods which they confiscate, and every fine whereby lesser crimes are punished, be assigned to themselves only, yet on this condition, that they may never compel anyone to confess by torture, and thus, pre-

caution enough will be taken against their being unfair to the commons, and through fear too lenient to the patricians. For besides that this fear is tempered by avarice itself, and that veiled under the specious name of justice, they are also numerous, and vote, not openly, but by ballot, so that a man may be indignant at losing his case, but can have no reason to impute it to a particular person. Moreover the fear of the syndics will restrain them from pronouncing an inequitable, or at least absurd sentence, or from acting any of them treacherously, besides that in so large a number of judges there will always be one or two, that the unfair stand in awe of. Lastly, as far as the commons are concerned, they also will be adequately secured if they are allowed to appeal to the syndics, who, as I have said, are by law authorized to inquire, judge, and determine about the conduct of the judges. For it is certain that the syndics will not be able to escape the hatred of the patricians, and on the other hand, will always be most popular with the commons, whose applause they will try as far as they can to bid for. To which end, opportunity being given them, they will not fail to reverse sentences pronounced against the laws of the court, and to examine any judge, and to punish those that are partial, for nothing moves the hearts of a multitude more than this. Nor is it an objection, but, on the contrary, an advantage, that such examples can but rarely occur. For not to mention that that commonwealth is ill ordered where examples are daily made of criminals (as we showed Chap. V. Sec. 2), those events must surely be very rare that are most renowned by fame.

42. Those who are sent as governors to cities and provinces ought to be chosen out of the rank of senators, because it is the duty of senators to look after the fortifications of cities, the treasury, the military, etc. But those, who were sent to somewhat distant regions, would be unable to attend the senate,

and, therefore, those only are to be summoned from the senate itself, who are destined to cities founded on their native soil; but those whom they wish to send to places more remote are to be chosen out of those, whose age is consistent with senatorial rank. But not even thus do I think that the peace of the dominion will be sufficiently provided for, that is, if the neighbouring cities are altogether denied the right of vote, unless they are so weak, that they can be openly set at naught, which cannot surely be supposed. And so it is necessary, that the neighbouring cities be granted the right of citizenship, and that from every one of them twenty, or thirty, or forty chosen citizens (for the number should vary with the size of the city) be enrolled among the patricians, out of whom three, four, or five ought to be yearly elected to be of the senate, and one for life to be a syndic. And let those who are of the senate be sent with their syndic, to govern the city out of which they were chosen.

43. Moreover, judges are to be established in every city, chosen out of the patricians of that city. But of these I think it unnecessary to treat at length, because they concern not the foundations of this sort of dominion in particular.

44. In every council the secretaries and other officials of this kind, as they have not the right of voting, should be chosen from the commons. But as these, by their long practice of business, are the most conversant with the affairs to be transacted, it often arises that more deference than right is shown to their advice, and that the state of the whole dominion depends chiefly on their guidance: which thing has been fatal to the Dutch. For this cannot happen without exciting the jealousy of many of the noblest. And surely we cannot doubt, that a senate, whose wisdom is derived from the advice, not of senators, but of officials, will be most frequented by the sluggish, and the condition of this sort of dominion will be little

better than that of a monarchy directed by a few counsellors
of the king. (See Chap. VI. Secs. 5-7.) However, to this evil
the dominion will be more or less liable, according as it was
well or ill founded. For the liberty of a dominion is never defended without risk, if it has not firm enough foundations;
and, to avoid that risk, patricians choose from the commons
ambitious ministers, who are slaughtered as victims to appease
the wrath of those, who are plotting against liberty. But where
liberty has firm enough foundations, there the patricians themselves vie for the honour of defending it, and are anxious that
prudence in the conduct of affairs should flow from their own
advice only; and in laying the foundations of this dominion we
have studied above all these two points, namely, to exclude the
commons from giving advice as much as from giving votes
(Secs. 3, 4), and, therefore, to place the whole authority of the
dominion with the whole body of patricians, but its exercise
with the syndics and senate, and, lastly, the right of convoking
the senate, and treating of matters affecting the common welfare with consuls chosen from the senate itself. But, if it is
further ordained that the secretary, whether in the senate or
in other councils, be appointed for four or five years at most,
and have attached to him an assistant-secretary appointed for
the same period, to bear part of the work during that time,
or that the senate have not one, but several secretaries, employed
one in one department, and another in another, the power of
the officials will never become of any consequence.

45. Treasurers are likewise to be chosen from the commons,
and are to be bound to submit the treasury accounts to the
syndics as well as to the senate.

46. Matters concerning religion we have set forth at sufficient
length in our Theologico-Political Treatise.[3] Yet certain points
we then omitted, of which it was not there the place to treat;

[3] Above, pp. 48-73.

for instance, that all the patricians must be of the same religion, that is, of that most simple and general religion, which in that treatise we described. For it is above all to be avoided, that the patricians themselves should be divided into sects, and show favour, some to this, and others to that, and thence become mastered by superstition, and try to deprive the subjects of the liberty of speaking out their opinions. In the second place, though everyone is to be given liberty to speak out his opinion, yet great conventicles are to be forbidden. And, therefore, those that are attached to another religion are, indeed, to be allowed to build as many temples as they please; yet these are to be small, and limited to a certain standard of size, and on sites at some little distance one from another. But it is very important, that the temples consecrated to the national religion should be large and costly, and that only patricians or senators should be allowed to administer its principal rites, and thus that patricians only be suffered to baptize, celebrate marriages, and lay on hands, and that in general they be recognized as the priests of the temples and the champions and interpreters of the national religion. But, for preaching, and to manage the church treasury and its daily business, let some persons be chosen from the commons by the senate itself, to be, as it were, the senate's deputies, and, therefore, bound to render it account of everything.

47. And these are points that concern the foundations of this sort of dominion; to which I will add some few others less essential indeed, but yet of great importance. Namely, that the patricians, when they walk, should be distinguished by some special garment, or dress, and be saluted by some special title; and that every man of the commons should give way to them; and that, if any patrician has lost his property by some unavoidable misfortune, he should be restored to his old condition at the public expense; but if, on the contrary, it be

proved that he has spent the same in presents, ostentation, gaming, debauchery, &c., or that he is insolvent, he must lose his dignity, and be held unworthy of every honour and office. For he, that cannot govern himself and his own private affairs, will much less be able to advise on public affairs.

48. Those, whom the law compels to take an oath, will be much more cautious of perjury, if they are bidden to swear by the country's safety and liberty and by the supreme council, than if they are told to swear by God. For he who swears by God, gives as surety some private advantage to himself, whereof he is judge; but he, who by his oath gives as surety his country's liberty and safety, swears by what is the common advantage of all, whereof he is not judge, and if he perjures himself, thereby declares that he is his country's enemy.

49. Academies, that are founded at the public expense, are instituted not so much to cultivate men's natural abilities as to restrain them. But in a free commonwealth arts and sciences will be best cultivated to the full, if everyone that asks leave is allowed to teach publicly, and that at his own cost and risk. But these and the like points I reserve for another place.[4] For here I determined to treat only such matters as concern an aristocratic dominion only.

---

[4] This promise is not kept by the author, no doubt owing to his not living to finish the work.

CHAPTER IX

OF ARISTOCRACY (*continuation*)

HITHERTO we have considered an aristocracy, so far as it takes its name from one city, which is the head of the whole dominion. It is now time to treat of that, which is in the hands of more than one city, and which I think preferable to the former. But that we may notice its difference and its superiority, we will pass in review the foundations of dominion, one by one, rejecting those foundations, which are unsuited to the present kind, and laying in their place others for it to rest upon.

2. The cities, then, which enjoy the right of citizenship, must be so built and fortified, that, on the one hand, each city by itself may be unable to subsist without the rest, and that yet, on the other hand, it cannot desert the rest without great harm to the whole dominion. For thus they will always remain united. But cities, which are so constituted, that they can neither maintain themselves, nor be dangerous to the rest, are clearly not independent, but absolutely subject to the rest.

3. But the contents of the ninth and tenth sections of the last chapter are deduced from the general nature of aristocracy, as are also the proportion between the numbers of the patricians and the multitude, and the proper age and condition of those that are to be made patricians; so that on these points no difference can arise, whether the dominion be in the hands of one or more cities. But the supreme council must here be on a different footing. For if any city of the dominion were assigned for the meeting of this supreme council, it would in reality

be the head of the dominion; and, therefore, either they would
have to take turns, or a place would have to be assigned for
this council, that has not the right of citizenship, and belongs
equally to all. But either alternative is as difficult to effect, as
it is easy to state; I mean, either that so many thousands of
men should have to go often outside their cities, or that they
should have to assemble sometimes in one place, sometimes in
another.

4. But that we may conclude aright what should be done in
this matter, and on what plan the councils of this dominion
ought to be formed, from its own very nature and condition,
these points are to be considered; namely, that every city has
so much more right than a private man, as it excels him in
power (Chap. II. Sec. 4), and consequently that every city of
this dominion has as much right within its walls, or the limits
of its jurisdiction, as it has power; and, in the next place, that
all the cities are mutually associated and united, not as under
a treaty, but as forming one dominion, yet so that every city
has so much more right as against the dominion than the
others, as it exceeds the others in power. For he who seeks
equality between unequals, seeks an absurdity. Citizens, indeed, are rightly esteemed equal, because the power of each,
compared with that of the whole dominion, is of no account.
But each city's power constitutes a large part of the power of
the dominion itself, and so much the larger, as the city itself
is greater. And, therefore, the cities cannot all be held equal.
But, as the power of each, so also its right should be estimated
by its greatness. The bonds, however, by which they should be
bound into one dominion, are above all a senate and a court
of justice (Chap. IV. Sec. 1). But how by these bonds they
are all to be so united, that each of them may yet remain, as
far as possible, independent, I will here briefly show.

5. I suppose then, that the patricians of every city, who,

according to its size, should be more, or fewer (Sec. 3), have supreme right over their own city, and that, in that city's supreme council, they have supreme authority to fortify the city and enlarge its walls, to impose taxes, to pass and repeal laws, and, in general, to do everything which they judge necessary to their city's preservation and increase. But to manage the common business of the dominion, a senate is to be created on just the same footing as we described in the last chapter, so that there be between this senate and the former no difference, except that this has also authority to decide the disputes, which may arise between cities. For in this dominion, of which no city is head, it cannot be done by the supreme council. (See Chap. VI. Sec. 38.)

6. But, in this dominion, the supreme council is not to be called together, unless there is need to alter the form of the dominion itself, or on some difficult business, to which the senators shall think themselves unequal; and so it will very rarely happen, that all the patricians are summoned to council. For we have said (Chap. VIII. Sec. 17), that the supreme council's function is to pass and repeal laws, and to choose the ministers of the dominion. But the laws, or general constitution of the whole dominion, ought not to be changed as soon as instituted. If, however, time and occasion suggest the institution of some new law or the change of one already ordained, the question may first be discussed in the senate, and after the agreement of the senate in the matter, then let envoys next be sent to the cities by the senate itself, to inform the patricians of every city of the opinion of the senate, and lastly, if the majority of the cities follow that opinion, it shall then remain good, but otherwise be of no effect. And this same order may be observed in choosing the generals of the army and the ambassadors to be sent to other realms, as also about decrees concerning the making of war or accepting conditions

of peace. But in choosing the other public officials, since (as we showed in Sec. 4) every city, as far as can be, ought to remain independent, and to have as much more right than the others in the dominion, as it exceeds them in power, the following order must necessarily be observed. The senators are to be chosen by the patricians of each city; that is, the patricians of one city are to elect in their own council a fixed number of senators from their colleagues of their own city, which number is to be that of the patricians of that city as one to twelve (Chap. VIII. Sec. 30); and they are to designate whom they will to be of the first, second, third, or other series; and in like manner the patricians of the other cities, in proportion to their number, are to choose more or fewer senators, and distribute them among the series, into a certain number of which we have said the senate is to be divided. (Chap. VIII. Sec. 34.) By which means it will result, that in every series of senators there will be found senators of every city, more or fewer, according to its size. But the presidents and vice-presidents of the series, being fewer in number than the cities, are to be chosen by lot by the senate out of the consuls, who are to be appointed first. The same order is to be maintained in appointing the supreme judges of the dominion, namely, that the patricians of every city are to elect from their colleagues in proportion to their number more or fewer judges. And so it will be the case, that every city in choosing officials will be as independent as possible, and that each, in proportion to its power, will have the more right alike in the senate and the court of justice; supposing, that is, that the order observed by senate and court in deciding public affairs, and settling disputes is such in all respects, as we have decribed it in the thirty-third and thirty-fourth sections of the last chapter.[1]

[1] So the text: but the court of justice is not described till the thirty-seventh and following sections of Chap. VIII.

7. Next, the commanders of battalions and military tribunes are also to be chosen from the patricians. For as it is fair, that every city in proportion to its size should be bound to levy a certain number of soldiers for the general safety of the whole dominion, it is also fair, that from the patricians of every city in proportion to the number of regiments, which they are bound to maintain, they may appoint so many tribunes, captains, ensigns, etc., as are needed to discipline that part of the military, which they supply to the dominion.

8. No taxes are to be imposed by the senate on the subjects; but to meet the expenditure, which by decree of the senate is ncessary to carry on public business, not the subjects, but the cities themselves are to be called to assessment by the senate, so that every city, in proportion to its size, should pay a larger or smaller share of the expense. And this share indeed is to be exacted by the patricians of every city from their own citizens in what way they please, either by compelling them to an assessment, or, as is much fairer, by imposing taxes on them.

9. Further, although all the cities of this dominion are not maritime, nor the senators summoned from the maritime cities only, yet may the same emoluments be awarded to the senators, as we mentioned in the thirty-first section of the last chapter. To which end it will be possible to devise means, varying with the composition of the dominion, to link the cities to one another more closely. But the other points concerning the senate and the court of justice and the whole dominion in general, which I delivered in the last chapter, are to be applied to this dominion also. And so we see, that in a dominion which is in the hands of several cities, it will not be necessary to assign a fixed time or place for assembling the supreme council. But for the senate and court of justice a place is to be appointed in a village, or in a city, that has not the right of

voting. But I return to those points, which concern the cities taken by themselves.

10. The order to be observed by the supreme council of a single city, in choosing officials of the dominion and of the city, and in making decrees, should be the same that I have delivered in the twenty-seventh and thirty-sixth sections of the last chapter. For the policy is the same here as it was there. Next a council of syndics is to be formed, subordinate to the council of the city, and having the same relation to it as the council of syndics of the last chapter had to the council of the entire dominion, and let its functions within the limits of the city be also the same, and let it enjoy the same emoluments. But if a city, and consequently the number of its patricians be so small that it cannot create more than one syndic or two, which two are not enough to make a council, then the supreme council of the city is to appoint judges to assist the syndics in trials according to the matter at issue, or else the dispute must be referred to the supreme council of syndics. For from every city some also out of the syndics are to be sent to the place where the senate sits, to see that the constitution of the whole dominion is preserved unbroken, and they are to sit in the senate without the right of voting.

11. The consuls of the cities are likewise to be chosen by the patricians of their city, and are to constitute a sort of senate for it. But their number I cannot determine, nor yet do I think it necessary, since the city's business of great importance is transacted by its supreme council, and matters concerning the whole dominion by the great senate. But if they be few, it will be necessary that they give their votes in their council openly, and not by ballot, as in large councils. For in small councils, when votes are given secretly, by a little extra cunning one can easily detect the author of every vote, and in many ways deceive the less attentive.

12. Besides, in every city judges are to be appointed by its supreme council, from whose sentence, however, let everyone but an openly convicted criminal or confessed debtor have a right of appeal to the supreme court of justice of the dominion. But this need not be pursued further.

13. It remains, therefore, to speak of the cities which are not independent. If these were founded in an actual province or district of the dominion, and their inhabitants are of the same nation and language, they ought of necessity, like villages, to be esteemed parts of the neighbouring cities, so that each of them should be under the government of this or that independent city. And the reason of this is, that the patricians are chosen by the supreme council, not of the dominion, but of every city, and in every city are more or fewer, according to the number of inhabitants within the limits of its jurisdiction (Sec. 5). And so it is necessary, that the multitude of the city, which is not independent, be referred to the census of another which is independent, and depend upon the latter's government. But cities captured by right of war, and annexed to the dominion, are either to be esteemed associates in the dominion, and though conquered put under an obligation by that benefit, or else colonies to enjoy the right of citizenship are to be sent thither, and the natives removed elsewhere or utterly destroyed.

14. And these are the things, which touch the foundations of the dominion. But that its condition is better than that of the aristocracy, which is called after one city only, I conclude from this, namely, that the patricians of every city, after the manner of human desire, will be eager to keep, and if possible increase their right, both in their city and in the senate; and therefore will try, as far as possible, to attract the multitude to themselves, and consequently to make a stir in the dominion by good deeds rather than by fear, and to increase their own

number; because the more numerous they are, the more senators they will choose out of their own council (Sec. 6), and
hence the more right (Sec. 6) they will possess in the dominion.
Nor is it an objection, that while every city is consulting its
own interest and suspecting the rest, they more often quarrel
among themselves, and waste time in disputing. For if, while
the Romans are debating, Saguntum is lost: on the other
hand, while a few are deciding everything in conformity with
their own passions only, liberty and the general good are lost.
For men's natural abilities are too dull to see through everything at once; but by consulting, listening, and debating, they
grow more acute, and while they are trying all means, they at
last discover those which they want, which all approve, but
no one would have thought of in the first instance. But if anyone retorts, that the dominion of the Dutch has not long
endured without a count or one to fill his place, let him have
this reply, that the Dutch thought, that to maintain their
liberty it was enough to abandon their count, and to behead
the body of their dominion, but never thought of remoulding
it, and left its limbs, just as they had been first constituted,
so that the country of Holland has remained without a count,
like a headless body, and the actual dominion has lasted on
without the name. And so it is no wonder that most of its
subjects have not known, with whom the authority of the
dominion lay. And even had this been otherwise, yet those
who actually held dominion were far too few to govern the
multitude and suppress their powerful adversaries. Whence it
has come to pass, that the latter have often been able to plot
against them with impunity, and at last to overthrow them.
And so the sudden overthrow of the said republic [2] has not

---

[2] A.D. 1672. William Henry, Prince of Orange, afterwards William III.
of England, was made Statholder by a popular insurrection, consequent
on the invasion of the French.

arisen from a useless waste of time in debates, but from the misformed state of the said dominion and the fewness of its rulers.

15. This aristocracy in the hands of several cities is also preferable to the other, because it is not necessary, as in the first described, to provide against its whole supreme council being overpowered by a sudden attack, since (Sec. 9) no time or place is appointed for its meeting. Moreover, powerful citizens in this dominion are less to be feared. For where several cities enjoy liberty, it is not enough for him, who is making ready his way to dominion, to seize one city, in order to hold dominion over the rest. And, lastly, liberty under this dominion is common to more. For where one city reigns alone, there the advantage of the rest is only so far considered, as suits that reigning city.

CHAPTER X

OF ARISTOCRACY (*conclusion*)

I

HAVING explained and made proof of the foundations of both kinds of aristocracy, it remains to inquire whether by reason of any fault they are liable to be dissolved or changed into another form. The primary cause, by which dominions of this kind are dissolved, is that, which that most acute Florentine [1] observes in his "Discourses on Livy" (Bk. iii. Chap. I.), namely, that like a human body, "a dominion has daily added to it something that at some time or other needs to be remedied." And so, he says, it is necessary for something occasionally to occur, to bring back the dominion to that first principle, on which it was in the beginning established. And if this does not take place within the necessary time, its blemishes will go on increasing, till they cannot be removed, but with the dominion itself. And this restoration, he says, may either happen accidentally, or by the design and forethought of the laws or of a man of extraordinary virtue. And we cannot doubt, that this matter is of the greatest importance, and that, where provision has not been made against this inconvenience, the dominion will not be able to endure by its own excellence, but only by good fortune; and on the other hand that, where a proper remedy has been applied to this evil, it will not be possible for it to fall by its own fault, but only by some inevitable fate, as we shall presently show more

[1] Machiavelli.

clearly. The first remedy, that suggested itself for this evil, was
to appoint every five years a supreme dictator for one or two
months, who should have the right to inquire, decide, and
make ordinances concerning the acts of the senators and of
every official, and thereby to bring back the dominion to its
first principle. But he who studies to avoid the inconveniences,
to which a dominion is liable, must apply remedies that suit
its nature, and can be derived from its own foundations; otherwise in his wish to avoid Charybdis he falls upon Scylla. It
is, indeed, true that all, as well rulers as ruled, ought to be
restrained by fear of punishment or loss, so that they may not
do wrong with impunity or even advantage; but, on the other
hand, it is certain, that if this fear becomes common to good
and bad men alike, the dominion must be in the utmost danger.
Now as the authority of a dictator is absolute, it cannot fail
to be a terror to all, especially if, as is here required, he were
appointed at a stated time, because in that case every ambitious
man would pursue this office with the utmost energy; and it is
certain that in time of peace virtue is thought less of than
wealth, so that the more haughty a man he is, the more
easily he will get office. And this perhaps is why the Romans
used to make a dictator at no fixed time, but under pressure
of some accidental necessity. Though for all that, to quote
Cicero's words, "the tumour of a dictator was displeasing to
the good." [2] And to be sure, as this authority of a dictator
is quite royal, it is impossible for the dominion to change into
a monarchy without great peril to the republic, although it
happen for ever so short a time. Furthermore, if no fixed time
were appointed for creating a dictator, no notice would be paid
to the interval between one dictator and another, which is
the very thing that we said was most to be observed; and the

---

[2] Cic. ad Quint. Grat. iii. 8, 4. The better reading is "rumour," not
"tumour." "The good" in such a passage means the aristocratic party.

whole thing would be exceedingly vague, and therefore easily neglected. Unless, then, this authority of a dictator be eternal and fixed, and therefore impossible to be conferred on one man without destroying the form of dominion, the dictatorial authority itself, and consequently the safety and preservation of the republic will be very uncertain.

2. But, on the other hand, we cannot doubt (Chap. VI. Sec. 3), that, if without destroying the form of dominion, the sword of the dictator might be permanent, and only terrible to the wicked, evils will never grow to such a pitch, that they cannot be eradicated or amended. In order, therefore, to secure all these conditions, we have said, that there is to be a council of syndics subordinate to the supreme council, to the end that the sword of the dictator should be permanent in the hands not of any natural person, but of a civil person, whose members are too numerous to divide the dominion amongst themselves (Chap. IX. Secs. 1, 2), or to combine in any wickedness. To which is to be added, that they are forbidden to fill any other office in the dominion, that they are not the paymasters of the soldiery, and, lastly, that they are of an age to prefer actual security to things new and perilous. Wherefore the dominion is in no danger from them, and consequently they cannot, and in fact will not be a terror to the good, but only to the wicked. For as they are less powerful to accomplish criminal designs, so are they more so to restrain wickedness. For, not to mention that they can resist it in its beginnings (since the council lasts for ever), they are also sufficiently numerous to dare to accuse and condemn this or that influential man without fear of his enmity; especially as they vote by ballot, and the sentence is pronounced in the name of the entire council.

3. But the tribunes of the commons at Rome were likewise regularly appointed; but they were too weak to restrain the

power of a Scipio, and had besides to submit to the senate their plans for the public welfare,[3] which also frequently eluded them, by contriving that the one whom the senators were least afraid of should be most popular with the commons. Besides which, the tribunes' authority was supported against the patricians by the favour of the commons, and whenever they convoked the commons, it looked as if they were raising a sedition rather than assembling a council. Which inconveniences have certainly no place in the dominion which we have described in the last two chapters.

4. However, this authority of the syndics will only be able to secure the preservation of the form of the dominion, and thus to prevent the laws from being broken, or anyone from gaining by transgressing; but will by no means suffice to prevent the growth of vices, which cannot be forbidden by law, such as those into which men fall from excess of leisure, and from which the ruin of a dominion not uncommonly follows. For men in time of peace lay aside fear, and gradually from being fierce savages become civilized or humane, and from being humane become soft and sluggish, and seek to excel one another not in virtue, but in ostentation and luxury. And hence they begin to put off their native manners and to put on foreign ones, that is, to become slaves.

5. To avoid these evils many have tried to establish sumptuary laws; but in vain. For all laws which can be broken without any injury to another, are counted but a laughing-stock, and are so far from bridling the desires and lusts of men, that on the contrary they stimulate them. For "we are ever eager for forbidden fruit, and desire what is denied." Nor do idle men ever lack ability to elude the laws which are

---

[3] Not by law, except before B.C. 287 and in the interval between the dictatorship of Sulla and the consulship of Pompey and Crassus. But in the golden age of the republic the senate in fact controlled the tribunes.

instituted about things, which cannot absolutely be forbidden, as banquets, plays, ornaments, and the like, of which only the excess is bad; and that is to be judged according to the individual's fortune, so that it cannot be determined by any general law.

6. I conclude, therefore, that the common vices of peace, of which we are here speaking, are never to be directly, but indirectly forbidden; that is, by laying such foundations of dominion, that the result may be, that the majority, I do not say are anxious to live wisely (for that is impossible), but are guided by those passions whence the republic has most advantage. And therefore the chief point to be studied is, that the rich may be, if not thrifty, yet avaricious. For there is no doubt, that, if this passion of avarice, which is general and lasting, be encouraged by the desire of glory, most people would set their chief affection upon increasing their property without disgrace, in order to acquire honours, while avoiding extreme infamy. If then we examine the foundations of both kinds of aristocracy which I have explained in the last two chapters, we shall see, that this very result follows from them. For the number of rulers in both is so large, that most of the rich have access to government and to the offices of the dominion open to them.

7. But if it be further ordained (as we said, Chap. VIII. Sec. 47), that patricians who are insolvent be deposed from patrician rank, and that those who have lost their property by misfortune be restored to their former position, there is no doubt that all will try their best to keep their property. Moreover, they will never desire foreign costumes, nor disdain their native ones, if it is by law appointed, that patricians and candidates for office should be distinguished by a special robe, concerning which see Chap. VIII. Secs. 25, 47. And besides these, other means may be devised in every dominion agreeable

to the nature of its situation and the national genius, and herein it is above all to be studied, that the subjects may do their duty rather spontaneously than under pressure of the law.

8. For a dominion, that looks no farther than to lead men by fear, will be rather free from vices, than possessed of virtue. But men are so to be led, that they may think that they are not led, but living after their own mind, and according to their free decision; and so that they are restrained only by love of liberty, desire to increase their property, and hope of gaining the honours of the dominion. But effigies, triumphs, and other incitements to virtue, are signs rather of slavery than liberty. For rewards of virtue are granted to slaves, not freemen. I admit, indeed, that men are very much stimulated by these incitements; but, as in the first instance, they are awarded to great men, so afterwards, with the growth of envy, they are granted to cowards and men swollen with the extent of their wealth, to the great indignation of all good men. Secondly, those, who boast of their ancestors' effigies and triumphs, think they are wronged, if they are not preferred to others. Lastly, not to mention other objections, it is certain that equality, which once cast off the general liberty is lost, can by no means be maintained, from the time that peculiar honours are by public law decreed to any man renowned for his virtue.

9. After which premisses, let us now see whether dominions of this kind can be destroyed by any cause to which blame attaches. But if any dominion can be everlasting, that will necessarily be so, whose constitution being once rightly instituted remains unbroken. For the constitution is the soul of a dominion. Therefore, if it is preserved, so is the dominion. But a constitution cannot remain unconquered, unless it is defended alike by reason and common human passion: otherwise, if it relies only on the help of reason, it is certainly weak and easily overcome. Now since the fundamental constitution

of both kinds of aristocracy has been shown to agree with reason and common human passion, we can therefore assert that these, if any kinds of dominion, will be eternal, in other words, that they cannot be destroyed by any cause to which blame attaches, but only by some inevitable fate.

10. But it may still be objected to us, that, although the constitution of dominion above set forth is defended by reason and common human passion, yet for all that it may at some time be overpowered. For there is no passion, that is not sometimes overpowered by a stronger contrary one; for we frequently see the fear of death overpowered by the greed for another's property. Men, who are running away in panic fear from the enemy, can be stopped by the fear of nothing else, but throw themselves into rivers, or rush into fire, to escape the enemy's steel. In whatever degree, therefore, a commonwealth is rightly ordered, and its laws well made; yet in the extreme difficulties of a dominion, when all, as sometimes happens, are seized by a sort of panic terror, all, without regard to the future or the laws, approve only that which their actual fear suggests, all turn towards the man who is renowned for his victories, and set him free from the laws, and (establishing thereby the worst of precedents), continue him in command, and entrust to his fidelity all affairs of state: and this was, in fact, the cause of the destruction of the Roman dominion. But to answer this objection, I say, first, that in a rightly constituted republic such terror does not arise but from a due cause. And so such terror and consequent confusion can be attributed to no cause avoidable by human foresight. In the next place, it is to be observed, that in a republic such as we have above described, it is impossible (Chap. VIII. Secs. 9, 25), for this or that man so to distinguish himself by the report of his virtue, as to turn towards himself the attention of all, but he must have many rivals favoured by others. And

so, although from terror there arise some confusion in the republic, yet no one will be able to elude the law and declare the election of anyone to an illegal military command, without its being immediately disputed by other candidates; and to settle the dispute, it will, in the end, be necessary to have recourse to the constitution ordained once for all, and approved by all, and to order the affairs of the dominion according to the existing laws. I may therefore absolutely assert, that as the aristocracy, which is in the hands of one city only, so especially that which is in the hands of several, is everlasting, or, in other words, can be dissolved or changed into another form by no internal cause.

Chapter XI

Of Democracy

I

I PASS, at length, to the third and perfectly absolute dominion, which we call democracy. The difference between this and aristocracy consists, we have said, chiefly in this, that in an aristocracy it depends on the supreme council's will and free choice only, that this or that man is made a patrician, so that no one has the right to vote or fill public offices by inheritance, and that no one can by right demand this right, as is the case in the dominion, whereof we are now treating. For all, who are born of citizen parents, or on the soil of the country, or who have deserved well of the republic, or have accomplished any other conditions upon which the law grants to a man right of citizenship; they all, I say, have a right to demand for themselves the right to vote in the supreme council and to fill public offices, nor can they be refused it, but for crime or infamy.

2. If, then, it is by a law appointed, that the elder men only, who have reached a certain year of their age, or the first-born only, as soon as their age allows, or those who contribute to the republic a certain sum of money, shall have the right of voting in the supreme council and managing the business of the dominion; then, although on this system the result might be, that the supreme council would be composed of fewer citizens than that of the aristocracy of which we treated above, yet, for all that, dominions of this kind should be called de-

mocracies, because in them the citizens, who are destined to manage affairs of state, are not chosen as the best by the supreme council, but are destined to it by a law. And although for this reason dominions of this kind, that is, where not the best, but those who happen by chance to be rich, or who are born eldest, are destined to govern, are thought inferior to an aristocracy; yet, if we reflect on the practice or general condition of mankind, the result in both cases will come to the same thing. For patricians will always think those the best, who are rich, or related to themselves in blood, or allied by friendship. And, indeed, if such were the nature of patricians, that they were free from all passion, and guided by mere zeal for the public welfare in choosing their patrician colleagues, no dominion could be compared with aristocracy. But experience itself teaches us only too well, that things pass in quite a contrary manner, above all, in oligarchies, where the will of the patricians, from the absence of rivals, is most free from the law. For there the patricians intentionally keep away the best men from the council, and seek for themselves such colleagues in it, as hang upon their words, so that in such a dominion things are in a much more unhappy condition, because the choice of patricians depends entirely upon the arbitrary will of a few, which is free or unrestrained by any law. But I return to my subject.

3. From what has been said in the last section, it is manifest that we can conceive of various kinds of democracy. But my intention is not to treat of every kind, but of that only, *wherein all, without exception, who owe allegiance to the laws of the country only, and are further independent and of respectable life, have the right of voting in the supreme council and of filling the offices of the dominion.* I say expressly, *who owe allegiance to the laws of the country only,* to exclude foreigners, who are treated as being under another's dominion.

I added, besides, *who are independent, except in so far as they are under allegiance to the laws of the dominion,* to exclude women and slaves, who are under the authority of men and masters, and also children and wards, as long as they are under the authority of parents and guardians. I said, lastly, *and of respectable life,* to exclude, above all, those that are infamous from crime, or some disgraceful means of livelihood.

4. But, perhaps, someone will ask, whether women are under men's authority by nature or institution? For if it has been by mere institution, then we had no reason compelling us to exclude women from government. But if we consult experience itself, we shall find that the origin of it is in their weakness. For there has never been a case of men and women reigning together, but wherever on the earth men are found, there we see that men rule, and women are ruled, and that on this plan, both sexes live in harmony. But on the other hand, the Amazons, who are reported to have held rule of old, did not suffer men to stop in their country, but reared only their female children, killing the males to whom they gave birth. But if by nature women were equal to men, and were equally distinguished by force of character and ability, in which human power and therefore human right chiefly consist; surely among nations so many and different some would be found, where both sexes rule alike, and others, where men are ruled by women, and so brought up, that they can make less use of their abilities. And since this is nowhere the case, one may assert with perfect propriety, that women have not by nature equal right with men: but that they necessarily give way to men, and that thus it cannot happen, that both sexes should rule alike, much less that men should be ruled by women. But if we further reflect upon human passions, how men, in fact, generally love women merely from the passion of lust, and esteem their cleverness and wisdom in proportion to the excel-

lence of their beauty, and also how very ill-disposed men are to suffer the women they love to show any sort of favour to others, and other facts of this kind, we shall easily see that men and women cannot rule alike without great hurt to peace. But of this enough.

[*The remainder is wanting.*]   *(1)*